NEVER A BAD DAY

BY BOB BABBITT

Meyer & Meyer Sport

British Library Cataloguing in Publication Data
A catalogue record for this book is available from the British Library

Never a bad day
Maidenhead: Meyer & Meyer Sport (UK) Ltd., 2013
ISBN: 978-1-78255-030-3

© 2013 by Meyer & Meyer Sport (UK) Ltd.
Auckland, Beirut, Budapest, Cairo, Cape Town, Dubai, Hägendorf, Indianapolis,
Maidenhead, Singapore, Sydney, Tehran, Wien
Member of the World Sport Publishers' Association (WSPA)
Printed by: Color House Graphics
ISBN: 978-1-78255-030-3
E-Mail: info@m-m-sports.com
www.m-m-sports.com

CONTENTS

INTRODUCTION 8

CHAPTER ONE – MEMORIES **12**
A DANCE THROUGH TIME 12
BOXING LESSONS 13
PIANO LESSONS 15
TRAINING WHEELS 17
ICE WAS NICE 18
ALWAYS GO TO THE STICK SIDE...20
ATHOUSAND MILES...23
"YOU... WILL... GET... TALLER."..24
AN ALL-STAR GAME WITH DAD 26
BASEBALL CARDS & CLASSIC TRIATHLONS 28

CHAPTER TWO – THE TRI LIFE..**32**
WHY TRI? 32
TRI 101 34
WHAT I'VE LEARNED 35
TIPS FROM THE BOTTOM 36
EVERYONE IN THE POOL...37
IT'S ALL ABOUT STYLE 38
THE EQUALIZER..40
LIFE IN A BUBBLE 41
MY CAMELOT 43
IRON JOURNEY...44

CHAPTER THREE – PRICELESS NUGGETS **48**
TIDBITS TO LIVE BY..48
SAVOR THE LITTLE THINGS 50
MY THOUGHTS ON "TRAINING" 51
WHY IT'S GOOD TO BE BAD 53
TAKING IT FROM SPORTS...54
BABBITTVILLE..56

CHAPTER FOUR – ALL IN FUN...**60**

RAT TALES 60

THANK YOU . . . THANK YOU VERY MUCH 62

THANK YOU . . . THANK YOU VERY MUCH – PART 2 63

MAKE MY DAY 64

"MAH" HORSE 66

AN E-TICKET RIDE 68

LONDON CALLING...71

KNUCKLEHEAD MOMENTS 72

MR. ED EXTRAVAGANZA 74

THE DIRTY DOZEN 77

MY BUCKET LIST . . . NOT! 79

CHAPTER FIVE – PERSEVERANCE......................................**82**

HE SHOCKED THE WORLD 82

LUCKY 13 83

FEAR THE KNIGHT..84

"I GET TO RIDE MY BIKE TODAY" 87

MILE MARKER 86 88

CATALINA MAN..91

NO LIMITS 93

CHAPTER SIX – INSPIRING **98**

HOPE...98

CHANGING A NATION FOREVER 99

ONE-ARM WILLIE..101

FLAMINGO TIME 103

40 DIAPERS A DAY 104

MR. CLUTCH 106

LIVING THE DREAM 108

CHAPTER SEVEN – MIRACLES **112**

TAZ THE WONDER DOG 112

RAISIN' THE BAR..114

THE DEFENDER...115

CHAPTER EIGHT – MILITARY HEROES **120**
A SALUTE TO HIS SOLDIERS...120
A WARRIOR FOR THE FALLEN 122
BOOTS AND UTES 124
"DON'T EVER GIVE UP" 125
A BLESSING 127

CHAPTER NINE – LEGENDARY **132**
"PRE" AND ROD...132
A TAINTED MEMORY 134
THE HOLY GRAIL 135
OUTKICKED BY A 14-YEAR-OLD 139
ONE AND DONE 140
MEANT TO BE 142
DAVE SCOTT'S SIGNATURE STYLE 143
PLAYING CATCH ON THE QUEEN K 144
WHY NOT DROP OUT?...146
CHICKEN SOUP AND A GLOW STICK 148
BULLY A BULLY 149
AN IRON GENT 151
THANKS FOR BELIEVING..152

CHAPTER TEN – GONE BUT NOT FORGOTTEN...........................**156**
UNBREAKABLE SPIRIT 156
THE BLAZEMAN 158
"LIVE LIKE KLAUS" 160
A MAN WELL LOVED 163
THE PROMISE 165
MR. LUCKY 166

ABOUT THE AUTHOR..**170**

CREDITS..**170**

FURTHER READING..**172**

INTRODUCTION

From the age of 9, I lived in Wilmette, a small suburb north of Chicago. I grew up playing recreational baseball, football and basketball and, while I had absolutely no skills whatsoever in any of those sports, I did have an ability to get the kids from my block together for semi-organized games in the street in front of our houses. Now some might think it would be a no-brainer to get kids out to play, but I'm here to tell you that it's a bit of an art form.

If I stop by your house and ask you to come out and play some baseball, the first question you're asking is a simple one: Who else is playing? No big deal if I've got a group already committed, but if yours is the first house I've approached I have to be a tad creative. Even as a kid we all want to be part of something cool. If no one else is there, you're just another dweeb with a baseball glove.

"Jimmy, Johnny, Darren and four others are in," I'd insist. "Grab your bat and your glove and meet us out there."

Now I've got to get quickly over to the other guys' houses and have them buy in as well. I was the organizer, the guy who always arranged the games and gathered the players. It was a role I happened to excel at, and a role I have embraced every day since.

When I moved to San Diego in 1978 and created a physical education program at a small private school, we didn't have large fields to play ball on, so I moved away from traditional sports and fell in love with running, swimming, cycling and a brand new sport called triathlon.

When I flew to Hawaii and finished the 1980 Ironman Triathlon, the third running of that event, I knew that my life had been changed forever. I felt like completing that event – which I was totally unprepared for – gave me a business card that I would carry with me for life. That card, based on finishing 2.4 miles of swimming, 112 miles of cycling and 26.2 miles of running all in a single day, would allow me to take on any challenges that came my way and to conquer any task that looked to be too ridiculous for me to overcome.

Finishing the Ironman gave me the courage to leave my job as a teacher and, along with my dearest friend, Lois Schwartz, the art teacher at that small private school, to eventually create a magazine called *Competitor* that would showcase the athletes, the personalities and the events that Lois and I had grown to love so much.

We didn't rely on focus groups or statistics or someone with an MBA. Nope. We relied on our gut even though the sports we chose to cover were about as non-mainstream as humanly possible.

Over time, we expanded *Competitor* magazine to numerous publications around the country, added a weekly radio show called The Competitors and an awards gala called The Competitor Magazine Endurance Sports Awards. Our goal was to make something big out of something small. We believed in our heart and soul that what we were doing was right, even if advertisers sometimes chose to ignore our pitch.

But we hung tough and eventually big business started to realize that the world of endurance sports is a huge one. Now the small company that Lois and I created back in 1987 is called The Competitor Group and underneath that large umbrella are the Rock 'N' Roll Marathon Series, The Muddy Buddy Ride and Run Series, The Tri Rock Triathlon Series, A Woman's Half Marathon Series plus *Competitor, Triathlete, Inside Triathlon, Velo* and *Women's Running* magazines – along with a ton of websites.

When I first came to California, my goals were simple: I was hoping to never hold a 9 to 5 job, never work at something that wasn't my passion, and to wear shorts to work as many days as possible. I am proud to say that I have been successful at all three.

When I speak to groups from time to time about the growth of endurance sports since the creation of *Competitor* magazine, I like to finish up by telling the story of a young man named Michael Collins, the son of the creators of the Ironman Triathlon, Commander John and Judy Collins.

Michael raced in the 1979 Ironman, the second edition of the event, when it was still on the island of Oahu. There were no time limits back then, Michael was only 16 years old and, after mechanical problems and much, much more, Michael ended up taking over 24 hours to finish the race.

Flash ahead to 1997. Michael and I are standing at the Ironman finish line in Kona, Hawaii, as people streamed across the line. Yes, the race was still an adventure and a long day for many, but for those who dedicated themselves to actually training for the event, they were able to have time goals for race day.

One after another, the athletes would come across the finish line, look at their watches, shake their heads and kick the ground in disgust. Their goal had been to go 11:20 and they had gone 11:30. Or their goal was 12 hours and they went 12:15. "Crap," they'd yell, "I had a bad day!"

Michael turned to me and, without hesitating, said the following:

"These people have no idea," he insisted. "You know what a bad day is? A bad day is when you're out walking the Ironman marathon, you've been out there over 24 hours, the paper boy is coming by and he's delivering the paper with results of a race you're still in. Now THAT'S a bad day!"

Fortunately for me, because of the wonderful world of endurance sports and the people who have embraced it, my life has been this awesome journey filled with friends, family, memories and, of course, nothing but great days.

Bob Babbitt
@bob_babbitt

CHAPTER 1

*Jack and
Jeanne Babbitt*

MEMORIES

A DANCE THROUGH TIME

BOXING LESSONS

PIANO LESSONS

TRAINING WHEELS

ICE WAS NICE

ALWAYS GO TO THE STICK SIDE

A THOUSAND MILES

"YOU . . . WILL . . . GET . . . TALLER."

AN ALL-STAR GAME WITH DAD

BASEBALL CARDS & CLASSIC
TRIATHLONS

CHAPTER 1 – MEMORIES

"My dad taught me some of life's most important lessons with these gloves. He taught me, among other things, to stay calm in the heat of battle and to hit what you aim at."

Bob Babbitt

A DANCE THROUGH TIME

(A Tribute to Mom and Dad's 65th Anniversary)

It was only 6 p.m., but she was already in bed.

"I was so busy every day that by the time it started to get dark, I had a hard time keeping my eyes open," remembers Jeanne.

Just as she was about to doze off, her sister Dorothy burst into the room to tell her that their Aunt Rosie and Uncle Sam were on their way over to take them to a dance at the Kramer Hotel. Jeanne quickly changed, jumped into the Buick and headed off to the dance. Not long after she arrived, a good-looking young man with jet-black hair, a ready laugh and twinkling blue eyes approached the pretty 17-year-old.

"He introduced himself as Jack Green and asked if he could dance with me," remembers Jeanne with a smile.

She accepted, and their hands touched for the very first time. It was a meeting that would change their lives forever.

Among his friends, Jack was known as the D.D., the Designated Dancer. He had actually danced professionally for a time.

"My friends Teddy and Maury didn't dance, but they liked to meet girls," recalls Jack. "Teddy would say, 'I'd like to meet that girl in the blue,' so I'd go over, dance with her and then bring her over to meet my friend Teddy. Then Maury would say 'I'd like to meet the girl in the pink,' and I'd do the same thing with Maury."

The three buddies liked to have a little bit of fun, so they preferred to travel incognito. That's why they never gave their real last names when they were out on the town. Usually Jack went by Mr. Green, Teddy was Mr. White and Maury was Mr. Black.

"Sometimes we'd forget who was who," laughs Jack. "It changed from night to night."

But this night was different. Jack knew Jeanne was something special. He wasn't about to introduce her to Maury or Ted or anyone else. She wasn't out of Jack's sight – or off his arm – all night long.

"While we were dancing, he asked me for a date," remembers Jeanne. "During that date he asked me to marry him."

Marry him? After one dance and halfway though one date?

"I had dated lots of girls," insists Jack. "I knew right away that this was the girl for me. Period. That was it. No question about it."

My dad Jack-you-can-call-me-Green Babbitt and my mom Jeanne waited a year after that chance encounter on a hotel dance floor in the winter of 1940 to seal the deal.

On February 16, 2006, they celebrated 65 years of marriage.

"Can I have this dance" became "Can I spend the rest of my life with you?" And what a life it's been – three kids (I'm the youngest), five grandchildren, six great-grandchildren and hundreds of friends. Plus, they passed on a zest for life that all of us share.

It's still there. You can see it in their eyes after 65 years, 23,725 days and 569,400 hours together – that same look of knowing, of wonder; that same instantaneous bond that they shared for the first time on that snowy evening in Chicago. It started with a trip across the dance floor and became a trip through the second half of the 20th century and beyond.

They may have aged, but their devotion to each other has not changed a bit. No one has ever cut in.

When you love each other, time becomes immaterial.

It just seems to jitterbug on by.

BOXING LESSONS

The ceiling above my head was a mere four feet high. The pavement my knees scraped against was raw and abusive. As a child, the crawl space under my parents' home was always one of my favorite places to be. It consisted of memories stored in rows and rows of boxes just waiting to be rediscovered.

My sister Judi, my brother Floyd and I all had dad-made wooden toy boxes with our names in script on the side. Floyd's, although 10 years older than mine, was still immaculate and well organized, just like its owner. Mine is missing two wheels and a fair amount of paint. Inside, there's a pile of cobweb-covered blue splinters with random pieces of long-forgotten games strewn among them.

I smiled and started rummaging through. Head pieces from the Rock 'Em Sock Em' Robots. My favorite game, electronic football (little magnetic guys and a cotton swab in the shape of a football), was still somewhat intact. Man, my friends and I could entertain ourselves for hours with that baby. Huddle up the players, tuck the cotton swab under one of their miniature arms, throw the switch and watch everyone scramble. Every time you switched the game on, every other electric appliance in the house switched off. Lucy, Desi, Fred and Ethel suddenly became an X-rated scramble. It was what you might call a maximum impact toy.

In a corner of my toy box, beneath some stuffed animals, was a pair of red boxing gloves I haven't seen in over 35 years. Suddenly, I'm 10 years old, back in the basement, facing my dad.

He circles to the right and leads with the left. Out of nowhere, a padded glove thuds against the side of my head. I stagger back, seeing small farm animals circling my forehead. There's the pig. Look at the size of that cow! In a fog, I try to remember my dad's instructions: "Keep your gloves up and protect your head," he told me over and over again. "Always protect your head." It's too much. My dental-floss-look-alike arms fight a losing battle, struggling to keep those mammoth red piles of padding aloft at head level, quivering from the effort.

Fathers and sons share a unique relationship. Most of our communication is of the barely spoken variety. When you're about four or five, a glove and a ball are introduced for the first time. Not a lot of dialogue comes along for the ride. "Let's throw" is what I remember. Further down the father-son timeline, dad introduces a full assortment of life's props with the same type of exciting banter. From the guys I've talked to, "Let's hit" accompanies a bat and usually occurs around the same time as "Let's throw." "Let's drive" and "Let's fill out these college applications" is still light years away.

I remember how the basement boxing started. I came home from school with a bloody nose after a scuffle of some sort. The next day, these red lace-up pillows entered my life. "Let's box," said my dad.

My dad worked late every night, so by the time he got home the rest of the family had already eaten. For the next year or so, every few weeks he appeared at my door after his dinner, gloves in hand. We would retire to the basement, silently tie them on, and then dance the pugilist tango. I was the original designated hittee, my dad the designated hitter. Left hands, right hands, combinations, uppercuts, body blows . . . to me the guy was a human octopus. The words were scarce, but they sunk in. "Block with the left . . . load up the right . . . protect the head."

I'd be breathing heavy from exhaustion and panic after just a few minutes and could never remember my cues. "Block the left? Lead with the right?" I could feel my heart pounding in my head, accompanied as always by his omnipresent right jab. After 10 minutes or so, my dad would realize I had no more left to give. He would put his arm around me and tell me how good I was doing. Good? I hadn't come close to hitting him. I was a sweaty mess and had red glove tattoos all over my anatomy.

Then one day it happened. We had been going at it for about five minutes or so. He circled left and threw a left hand. I blocked with my left and attacked with the loaded-up right. For the first time in my life, my glove actually made contact with something other than his gloves or air. I hit him in the left shoulder – a glancing blow to be sure, but a blow nonetheless. We both stopped and stood motionless. My body was heaving back and forth, the sweat dripping from my flattop into my eyes.

He smiled, blue eyes dancing, and started unlacing his gloves. Taking the hint, I unlaced mine. As always, he put his arm around me as we walked to the stairway and back upstairs. At the top of the steps, I turned right to my room and he headed back to his.

"Great shot," was the last thing I heard before he disappeared. We never boxed again.

Back in the crawl space, I held the gloves up to the 60-watt light bulb above me. They seemed to be in pretty good shape. My dad taught me some of life's most important lessons with these gloves. He taught me, among other things, to stay calm in the heat of battle and to hit what you aim at. I placed the gloves back in the corner of my toy box, crawled back towards the entrance and flicked off the light. My dad just happened to be walking past as I emerged. He smiled.

"Lunch?" he asked. Sounds good to me.

Thanks for the pounding and the lessons, Dad.

PIANO LESSONS

Mike Geier's throw from behind the Estrin's hedges was right on target. Mark Avrech, barreling towards the dirt spot in the street that served as second base, was a dead duck. I had the ball in my glove and enough time to read a book while waiting for him to get there. He was history. The third out was so obvious that the other guys had already tucked their gloves under their arms and were headed towards the Ford Fairlane that served as our dugout. We had decided that the Fairlane was the class car of the neighborhood because it was the only one we knew of with a hood ornament. It seemed that the driver, who I happened to be related to by birth, had hit a robin the day before and somehow it had become lodged in the radiator. Only its tiny head and beak were visible above the top of the hood. Not exactly a Jaguar, a Mercedes or a Rolls Royce flying lady, but hey, a hood ornament is a hood ornament, right?

So the guys were already on their way to the Fairlane when Mark Avrech decided he would try to dislodge the ball from the glove the best way he knew how, by dislodging my arm from my body. It was a good attempt, but after the collision – after we both hit the ground – the ball was still firmly in my glove, and he was still unequivocally out. He helped me to my feet, and as I trotted toward the Fairlane accompanied by the shouts of my teammates, the worst possible thing that can happen to a kid happened. "Bobby!" yelled my mom, "It's time for your piano lesson!"

Being the scumbuckets they were, all the guys gave me a rousing chorus of "Bob-by! Bob-by! Time to go play the pi-an-o!" in the most derisive tone they could come up with on such short notice.

Disappointed, I kicked at the street and mumbled something about moms being created for the sole purpose of ruining every kid's life. Then I grabbed my Johnny Antonelli autographed glove, my battered Cubs cap bent appropriately at the corners of the brim just like my hero Ernie "Let's Play Three Today" Banks and, head down, trotted back to the house. I had the same spring in my step as you'd expect from a convicted killer as he makes the final jaunt from death row to the electric chair.

Sitting at the piano waiting patiently was Mrs. Debelva, my instructor. The redeeming part of finishing the long walk to the electric chair is knowing that it's a one-shot deal. You never, ever have to do it again. Piano lessons, as I was beginning to find out, never end. The piano bench itself was slippery and rock hard, and Mrs. Debelva always smelled like some giant purple fruit that I never could identify. Every time I went to push one of the keys it was always the wrong one. The rest of my family appreciated my piano lessons and practice time as much as most of us would appreciate having Stevie Wonder drive us home. My brother invented the world's first Walkman in an attempt to deal with the racket. He took two transistor radios, put one over each ear, turned them up full blast, and secured them in place with a pair of earmuffs. He would walk around the house like that until he saw Mrs. Debelva's car pull away. My dad and sister would huddle together downstairs in the family room like they were in an air raid shelter waiting for the big one. They would keep the sound on the television set up full blast, hoping to somehow drown out the ear-splitting sounds that emanated from the living room.

My mother, though, was a real glutton for punishment. She would sit in a chair in the very same room with me and Mrs. Debelva. She would smile and hum along to the nonsense that I slammed out on a daily basis. My music was so bad that Sid Vicious would sound like one of the great masters by comparison. And, after driving the family home and listening to it, Stevie would have prayed to be deaf too. It's not overstating the point to say that I was the absolute worst piano player in the history of the world.

Fortunately for both me and the musical world, my brief career as a pianist was about to come to an end. Mrs. Debelva had fire-red hair and spoke with a clipped French accent with an emphasis on the last syllable. "Bobby!" she said, "Today we will play Popeye the Sailor Man! Are you ready? One . . . two . . . three . . . go!" A very short time later, after I had played the "I am Pop . . ." part of the song – even before my mom started humming and swaying to the beat – Mrs. Debelva did a nose dive on middle C. Boom! She was out cold, facedown on the keyboard. A quick look down gave a hint to the reason. The bone of my left forearm was protruding through the skin, a compound fracture that was the result of my sterling defensive play at second base just minutes before. In all the excitement of the tag and the death march home, my body had yet to inform me about the trauma to my arm. Unfortunately, Mrs. Debelva was the first one to spot the injury. My mom yelled out and, before I knew it, my dad and I were in the car with the funny-looking hood ornament going for help. After an hour of frantic driving, we found a hospital and my arm was put in a cast. My brother, of course, was elated that he didn't have to wear his earmuffs in August ever again. And, even after I healed up, no one ever mentioned taking piano lessons again. Years later, I heard that my mother suggested it once, but my dad vetoed the idea, saying something like, "Dear, don't you think that poor woman has suffered enough?"

It was true. Mrs. Debelva had suffered plenty. For me, though, the incident was a blessing in disguise. During the period when I had the cast on my arm, I was able to hit a baseball better than I ever have, before or since. I was almost upset when the doctor said it was time for the cast to come off.

The reason I have digressed back to a childhood injury is that right now I am sitting here with a funky brace around my neck and under both arms. I made the mistake of trying to do a Greg Louganis half-gainer off my bicycle seat into the pavement the other day without the benefit of a watery entry. My collarbone was broken in two places and the doctor said it will be four to six weeks before I can expect to go out and play again. And guess what he recommended when he gave me the diagnosis? "Bob," he said sincerely. "This might be a good time for you to pick up a new hobby. Have you ever given any thought to playing the piano?"

Gee doc, thanks for the idea; but I have to agree with my dad. I think the poor woman has suffered enough.

TRAINING WHEELS

"Okay, we can take those off now."

I have just finished swimming five 200-yard freestyle repeats. The water is invigorating, the pace manageable, and my lane mates and I are getting along just fine. Life is good.

The words come from up high, from the coach on deck. The sun is directly behind her, so as she speaks her face is a glowing orb. She reaches out for my pull buoy, that foam piece of heaven that you put between your legs to keep your butt up and your legs and feet from dragging. Real swimmers know how to kick. A lot of us swimmers-come-lately fight to stay above the waterline. Pull buoys are our saving grace in the pool and wetsuits do the same in open water. I cling to the pool's gutter hoping she will give up and go away. No such luck. My pull buoy is gone, and I will have to work to stay afloat.

Suddenly I am whisked back in time and am once again five years old.

The alley behind our Chicago apartment building was runway-model narrow and paved in jagged, bicycle-tire-eating fissures. As a kid, you wonder about stuff like sidewalk and road cracks. Is someone buried underneath them? Will some cement-entombed creature one day suddenly reach a grimy tentacle up through a gaping crevice and swallow your sister whole?

As a little brother, you can only hope.

Our living situation was somewhat special. My grandfather – whom we called Poppaboy – and grandmother lived across the hall, and I had aunts, uncles and cousins living both upstairs and downstairs. We were never short of playmates or babysitters.

I remember Poppaboy's whiskers scratching my face when he kissed me goodnight. More often than not, he'd slip the kids silver dollars whenever he came over. Obviously he – and the cash – were always welcome.

One day I "accidentally" tripped one of my cousins as she galloped by on one of those sticks with a horse head glued on top and was sentenced to two days of off-the-bike time. It was my parents' punishment of choice, because tooling through the alley on two wheels was my favorite thing to do.

A few days later, my penalty served, I ran to the backyard to mount my steed. My dad was waiting, a big smile on his face and a big wrench in his hand.

"Today's the day," he said.

The day? I wondered.

"Today we're taking off your training wheels and teaching you how to really ride a bike."

"I already know how to really ride a bike," I said to myself. "I'm happy, I'm safe, and what genius decided two wheels are better than four?"

But my dad was determined to take away my link to the upright world. He then voiced those same tragic words:

"OK, we can take those off now."

The argument makes sense. Without training wheels, I would eventually achieve two-wheeled independence. For us leg draggers, pull buoys are our training wheels. Without them – the subject of today's lesson – I would supposedly learn better balance and achieve aquatic independence.

I beg for just one more set with my friends, but the jig is up. I am forced to go it alone, to actually use my legs to stay afloat.

If Poppaboy were alive, he'd slip me a silver dollar for learning the proper way to swim. But if I had my druthers? I'd slip Poppaboy two shiny ones and swim off into the sunset, arms pulling, legs floating, butt hovering above the waterline, my beloved pull buoy firmly in place.

ICE WAS NICE

When I first moved to Southern California, I was amazed at the size of some of the houses and the yards, but what really blew me away were the driveways. The what? Yep, the driveways.

When you're a California native, a driveway is, well, a driveway. When you're from the Midwest, a driveway is something that needs to be shoveled every time it snows. A quarter-mile long uphill driveway? A major league payday.

That's why the winter of 1961 was so weird. I was 10 years old, the month was January and the weather was cold enough to make the tips of your ears tingle and for my buddy Mike Geier to do his famous I'm-going-to-drench-my-head-in-water-go-outside-and-watch-follicles-turn-into-popsicles icicle head imitation.

But even though we could break off chunks of Mike's hair on a daily basis, we were still awaiting our first snowfall. There were lots of clouds, lots of wind, lots of cold but no white stuff.

My spending money came with the first snowfall. Without it, I was a landscaper without lawns, a window washer without windows, Matthew McConaughey with his shirt on or Britney Spears as mother of the year. I needed and loved the snow, but the Big Guy in the sky wasn't cooperating.

I knew that cold weather was the necessary evil that went along with snow. And snow? Merely the greatest toy ever invented.

When I got older, snow, ice and cold quickly lost their appeal. Adults have to drive to work on slippery pavement, dig out of snowplow-induced 10 foot drifts, and watch the street salt and slush do a frenzied termite imitation to the side of the Buick. And, of course, adults have to wear those fancy go-to-work clothes that never, ever keep you warm.

Kids don't have those problems. All they have to do is put on 12 layers of clothes – none of it matching – and go frolic in the powder. They don't have a best-dressed award. Instead, there's the best snowball arm – the longest distance thrown and the most resourceful in a full-on snowball attack. That's important. The biggest bummer? Getting all your snowball battle gear on and then realizing you have to completely ungear and go to the bathroom.

In our Midwestern version of a street gang, every neighborhood had its own snow fort. We would gladly sacrifice our little brother, little sister – or both – to defend it. During school hours, there was an unwritten law that no one messed with anyone else's fort. As soon as that final bell rang though, everything – and every fort – was fair game.

A good snow fort could be six feet tall, ten feet long and eight feet wide. We'd cut peep-and-throw holes in the side of each fort and spend every waking hour making snowballs, fixing up cracks in the large snowball foundation (you could only do repairs on days when the snow was good packing) and loading up for the next battle. The game itself – the heart pounding in your chest during the chase, the redness in your cheeks after an enemy "face wash" – was all that mattered. Winning was sort of an unnecessary by-product.

Every once in a while a flurry of snowballs would hit near Mrs. Thelma Hector, who always seemed to be out walking her poodle Victor during full-scale attacks. She majored in the nasty stare, and her fashion preference was definitely a bizarre mixture of early Amish and classic Phantom of the Opera. She wore a black pointy hat and long black cape. It was sort of fun to bounce snowballs near her and Victor and then take off. The look was worth the ammo.

But this was 1961, our snowless winter. Every evening we looked skyward, hoping for snow-filled clouds. One evening, I remember things looked especially promising: full-on cloud cover. I went to bed that night excited, hoping that when I woke up everything would be blanketed in white.

As I tried to sleep, I heard a sound that was vaguely familiar but didn't seem appropriate. If this was March through October, rain would make sense. But it wasn't . . . and it didn't.

The next morning, I woke up to a picture postcard. It had rained all night, and then the water froze. The entire neighborhood looked like a glazed donut. Perfectly formed icicles hung from the trees and the roof. The sun reflected off the ice that covered my driveway and the streets. I had never seen anything like it. After taking two steps from my house, I slid all the way down the driveway on my chin. As I lay there facedown, I wondered if I could skate on this stuff. I ran in, laced up my hockey skates, grabbed my stick, slapped some electrical tape on it and hit the street.

Before I knew it, Mike Geier and I, along with all the boys from the "hood," were out there playing hockey in the street . . . on skates! It was a miracle. Our street had never, ever frozen solid before.

After a full eight hours of skating and laughing and scoring and face plants and bouncing pucks off the side of Mr. Estrin's Ford Galaxy 500, we all collapsed exhausted on the curb. As we sat with our elbows on our knees, wordlessly watching our breath come and go in the expanding shadow of the sun, it began to snow.

The snow was what we had been waiting so long for, but no one was jumping up and down. We all knew that playing hockey in the streets had been really special. We were replaying in our minds what would turn out to be a singular adventure in our lives.

Who woulda thunk it? Winter was just about to break down and finally give us snow − but we didn't care.

For the time being, ice was nice.

ALWAYS GO TO THE STICK SIDE

It's about two-foot square and has jagged edges on all four sides. Next to this small tuft of carpeting is a lumpy pile of weathered black electrical tape. Home is a small box where the carpeting rooms with Cuno Barrigan, Tommy Aaron and a few of baseball's other all-time great unknowns.

It's not often that carpeting can make me smile, but this piece always does − guaranteed.

We heard the door close and peered out through the drapes to watch my parents and our 1962 red Ford Fairlane 500 pull away. Alpine Lane was still shiny with ice, and you could see the small puffs of cold air coming out of the mouths of each passerby, sort of like the little word bubbles you see in cartoons. The frost on the window, the icicles and the quick movements of people bucking headwinds outside told us that inside was the place to be.

The coast was clear. My cousin Glen grabbed the pillows from the couch and shoved the bigger ones under his shirt and the smaller ones into the legs of his pants. I brought the electrical tape from the tool box and pulled a line of the black stuff around Glen's body to keep his chest protector in place. An aluminum pie plate with eye holes and a rubber band was hidden from view under the EZ Boy for just such an occasion. It was no longer a pie tin, though. It had become a cooler-than-cool hockey mask.

Glen grabbed his goalie stick, pulled on his mittens and pretended to skate in circles, just like Chicago Blackhawks goalie Glen Hall.

I, on the other hand, was working over my Bobby Hull-autographed, biggest-curve-on-the-face-of-the-earth hockey-stick-from-hell. The tennis balls appeared, and it was show time.

Glen and I had 45 minutes max to get in our game, hide all the evidence and get the room back to normal before my parents got back from lunch. I'd take 10 shots, he'd take 10 shots. The prize? BR for the week and double dessert. (BR meant Bragging Rights, and nothing made your chest puff more proudly than bragging rights.)

Cushions formed the sides and back of the goal. There were very few arguments about a goal being in or not. We knew. We both knew.

The shooter would emerge from the far bathroom, skim across the brown linoleum (a great sliding surface) and move into the carpeted part of the room. The goalie would smother any attempt to jam one in from close range, and long range shots were difficult because of the narrowness of the hallway. The best way to score was to build up some speed coming across the slick stuff and then either pound in a 12-foot slap shot or wrist one in from straight on.

Big G's weakness was his stick hand. The guy had a magnet on the left (his glove side), but he knew – and I knew – that he could be had with a low shot to the stick side.

Wordlessly, I glanced his way. He nodded his pie-pan-covered face, and I moved in for the kill. Out of the bathroom, push up across the vinyl, a low wrist shot glove side from the carpet . . . GOAAAAAALLLLLLL Bobby Hull! I PF-Flyered my way around the room as the crowd on our reel-to-reel tape deck went wild.

Big G swatted his pillow-encased shins with his stick, telling himself to bear down. I chuckled. He looked like a rotund marshmallow with a metal head.

Flash Gordon was on the television in the background. Soon we would break for the show's Grand Prize game. This consisted of a caller asking the host to turn over a particular planet and then either receiving the gift on the back or getting stiffed.

"I'll take Saturn, Jim," the caller would say.

"Congratulations!" replies Jim. "You just won a month's supply of Ovaltine!"

We watched because a few weeks before someone – in the age of live television – had called in and said, "I'd like to pick Uranus." Jim turned white and the show immediately went black. The next week, our favorite planet was missing when the show came back on the air.

Someone was picking Mars in the background, and I was picking on the Big G's glove side again.

Blackhawk star Stan Mikita said that sometimes you can become too predictable. I smiled to myself. Forget the big guy's weakness. I'm going right at him.

I was four out of seven when I got in a little too tight. Big G came up and out of the net, sliding right at me. I tried to lift the tennis ball over and wrist it toward the left post.

My stick stuck in the carpet and lifted out a two-foot-square patch of shag. We both froze. What do we do? Not a word was spoken.

Pie-pan face started to put all the pillows away and undo himself. I got out the black electrical tape and tried to assess the damage.

My mother is a vacuum-aholic. She could hum and vacuum all day long. Lint was the enemy, and she would seek it out relentlessly. Her Hoover would suck on this carpet until she sucked all the evidence into the hose.

This would be tough. We had to make this surgery mother-proof.

I took the piece of shag and tried to replace my divot. Stepping on it was not going to be enough.

There was no time for a major operation. I grabbed the square. Big G doubled up the tape, Flash Gordon crash-landed on some planet that looked oddly like the local forest preserve, and we jammed that puppy back into place.

When the Ford Fairlane pulled in, Big G and I were transfixed on the tube – our secret. Well, we had decided that it would remain our secret. My parents came downstairs, pulled up their chairs, and after a few minutes, made small talk, asking us if we thought people would ever travel in space like Flash Gordon.

Flash Gordon? Hell, we knew that if that tape ever came loose, the two of us would be the first 10-year-olds to orbit the moon.

Zoom ahead 20 years. My parents decide that they've lived on the Ponderosa since 1959 and that maybe it's time to remodel. New carpeting? Why not?

I was in town visiting and stood nearby as the old carpeting was rolled up. My mom wasn't even looking when a familiar piece of black tape came into view.

I guess we never, ever outgrow our parents. My heart rate went up, and I hoped nobody else would see.

What were they going to do, ground me?

I walked over and pulled quickly on the tape, removed the evidence and shoved it in my pocket.

As I was about to head upstairs, my dad walked over to the old carpet roll and noticed that there was a piece missing. He smiled and pointed my way.

"Slap shot or wrist shot?

"Wrist shot."

 "Good or no good?"

"Wide left."

"Always go to his stick side," he said shaking his head and smiling. "Big G is hopeless over there."

I guess there are certain givens in life. There's no sense in fighting it. First, parents know everything. Second, always replace your divots.

And third? When in doubt, always go to the stick side.

A THOUSAND MILES

(To Dad for Father's Day, 1988)

One thousand miles. It doesn't seem like much when you compare it to the mega-miles that most triathletes and cyclists put in over the span of 12 months. But for a 74-year-old former auto parts man, 1,000 miles in a year is one heck of an accomplishment.

You see, this gentleman is one of the many Americans who retire soon after their 65th birthday and then sit back to "enjoy the good life." The "good life" consists of a little traveling, a bunch of eating and a ton of driving the wife – who has never had him around the house during the daytime before – absolutely crazy.

What most retirees don't realize is that there is an identity attached to what they do for a living. The architect designs, the carpenter builds and the auto parts man sells. They all communicate and interact in a dynamic, exciting environment at least five days per week. Then they retire and have absolutely nothing. I take that back. They've got nothing but time.

Our auto parts man, rather than hustling around the auto parts store for 12 hours a day, suddenly finds himself on a diet of Phil and Oprah sprinkled around four meals a day. The day-to-day physical and emotional fitness of the working stiff is gone.

Friends and relatives try to get the recent retiree to stay active – to swim, to walk, to ride a stationary bike. But when you hang with other 65-year-olds who have the I-feel-like-hanging-around-because-I've-earned-the-right attitude, that's exactly what you do. You swap stories, recipes and channel changers.

Then it happens. The body, after years of moving fast, soon adjusts to life as a slug. In fact, the body enjoys going slow so much, it tries to slow down a little bit too much.

After eight years of retirement, the auto parts man recoils at the onslaught of what feels like a giant vise tightening across the middle of his chest. "It can't be happening to me," he says to himself. "Wait a minute; I'm going to start working out tomorrow. I swear."

It's too late. A heart attack is the great awakener. You can retire from business, you can sell your last oil filter, but fitness has to be forever. You simply cannot retire from staying active.

After the heart attack, the auto parts man not only turned over a new leaf he planted himself a whole new forest. After the heart attack, the doctors didn't need to remind him that being active is where it's at. He had ignored his know-almost-nothing son who had been telling him the same information for years. But now he bought the whole package and went after fitness with a vengeance. Now at 74, his day begins with six miles on the Schwinn Aerodyne. Early in the year, it was two days a week. Then four days. Now it's seven days religiously – 42 miles a week! In the last year he's gone four digits, turning the last clicker on Father's Day Eve. The breathless call came that morning. "Bob, I just turned 1,000!" I was as excited as he was. After all, the auto parts man is my dad.

One thousand miles! Hey, big guy, I'm proud of you. Happy Father's Day and keep spinning!

"YOU . . . WILL . . . GET . . . TALLER."

(For my dad before his knee surgery on August 9, 1990)

When I walked into the room, I looked past the washer and dryer and to the left of a freezer packed with enough frozen food to feed a small Latin American country for a month. Overhead, still hanging from the bare two-by-fours, was a pull-up bar that my dad put up when I was all of 15 years old. It was dusty and cluttered with more than its share of cobwebs. But when I slapped the old steel bar against my palms, it felt just like it did almost 25 years ago. The only difference was that I didn't need the use of a chair – or my dad – to reach it.

You see, when I was a little guy, I was a REAL little guy. All during high school I weighed 95 pounds soaking wet and stood barely five feet tall. In school pictures, I was forever the kid in the first row. There was a time I thought I'd never grow. But my dad didn't share that opinion. "You'll be fine," he'd say. "Just wait. One day, you'll be as tall as everyone else." Right.

In the meantime, Wednesday nights – which was Gus Giordan's dance class night at Locust Junior High in Wilmette, Illinois – would continue to be my personal Friday the 13th. Before class, the boys and girls would make two separate lines. Then, as we marched into the gymnasium – I mean, dance hall – we'd simply match up with whoever was next to us. It looked like one of those air-raid drills most of the time, with all the guys and girls scrambling to be with their favorites. I didn't have a favorite. I just wanted to avoid Jill Solomon, the biggest girl in the class; because I swore if she ever stepped wrong she would crush me like a grape.

But I *always* ended up with Jill Solomon. She had to be five feet, eight inches and 145 pounds. That might not sound like much to you, but you weren't the guy who needed a special pad on his car seat in order to go for his driver's license. Without the pad I was one with the dashboard, looking directly into the numbers on the speedometer. When the driver's education instructor told us to put the Rambler in gear, look out the windshield and get "the big picture," all I got was a big stiff neck from looking straight up.

So when we talk about dancing the cha-cha with a girl who's big enough to go one-on-one with the Fridge (former Chicago Bears football great William "The Refrigerator" Perry), I'm the first guy in town to ask for hazard pay.

When I went out for the wrestling team, there were two guys in the 98-pound division: Bob Mayer, who was the best guy in the district, and yours truly, who wasn't even the best in his own living room. My sister, Judi, could pin me anytime she wanted to. To add insult to injury, after she pinned my legs and arms down, she'd lick my nose. Ask Olympic Gold Medalist Dan Gable about the psychological ramifications of nose licking. He'll tell you there's nothing more humbling for a wrestler than to end up with a soggy nose – especially if that sogginess is inflicted by a girl.

Because of our lack of 98-pounders, I was forced to wrestle a guy who was in a similar predicament: He was the only heavyweight in the school. The coach thought this was a good idea because I could work on my strength by trying to lift a Volkswagen van off the mat while my partner could work on his speed. What the coach hadn't noticed was that besides being short and light, I was also slow. Most of our practices consisted of me making a move toward Gary Grieshaber's legs and then him falling down on top of me. To this day, I don't like being in tight places. Wrestling made me claustrophobic. I'm sure that's also why I have always hated working under a car. I guess I feel like I've already done plenty of time under a large, greasy chassis.

My worst nightmare during high school was that all the other guys would leave practice and this 245-pound behemoth would fall asleep on top of me and I would suffocate. Can you picture a worse death? I could see the headline: *"Boy Dies of Asphyxiation. Large Tub of Goo says, 'Sorry, I forgot he was there.'"*

My dad continued his ridiculous nonstop optimism. He told me to hang in there. Eventually I'd grow. I have to admit I was getting downright pessimistic. There were guys in my junior high with facial hair, chest hair and were close to six feet tall. I remember Larry Miller's parents (Larry had a full-on moustache in seventh grade) giving him a cigarette lighter when he graduated junior high. At the same time, I was still getting advanced weapons and camouflage gear for my G.I. Joe.

One day during my sophomore year of high school, I came home and my dad called me down to the basement. Hanging from the rafters of the utility room was this pull-up bar that he had obviously just installed. "I don't know if this will work or not," he said, pointing skyward. "But every day after school I want you to come home and hang from this bar." He paused for a second and then stretched out his last sentence for what seemed like an eternity: "You . . . will . . . get . . taller."

Who could argue with that logic? Certainly not me. I didn't miss too many days. My dad would give me a boost, and I'd just hang there, my face getting redder by the minute, calluses hardening on my palms, and my arms feeling like they were coming right out of their sockets. I figured I had absolutely nothing to lose. If I didn't grow soon, I knew I was destined to become a jockey, the eighth dwarf (those guys would have to call me Big Dude) or land the lead in *Peter Pan*. But time was running out.

After I graduated high school, I grew a bunch: six inches my first year of college and a couple more after that. I doubt if any of it was because of that pull-up bar, but I know that my dad's faith kept me from giving up.

My 75-year-old dad is about to have one of his knee joints replaced with a new-fangled aluminum one. For years, he's been limping around on an arthritic knee that I know has made his life tough to deal with. He's retired, but he likes to swim, ride his Schwinn Aerodyne, walk and play golf. At this point in time, he can't do any of the above without a lot of pain. What I particularly don't like is that his knee makes it hard for him to go for walks on the beach or hike around the neighborhood with his No. 2 son. He's an active guy whose knee hasn't allowed him to be active.

When I was a kid, all I wanted to be was taller. All my dad wants now is to be more mobile. I don't know why, but I have a gut feeling that in little time he'll be playing a mean game of golf and hitting the heck out of the driver and his fairway woods. I can't wait to have him out here next winter so we can walk the beach, and he can make up new how-I-reached-the-green-of-a-par-five-in-two-strokes stories.

Dad . . . Here's the payback from your No. 2 son. Every day after you return home from the hospital, you need to hit the weights and rehab that knee.

And you can take this to the bank, big guy:

You . . . will . . . get . . . more . . . mobile.

AN ALL-STAR GAME WITH DAD

(For Father's Day 1992)

It's a red pennant, bordered on one side with yellow. The ties that came with it are long gone. The names scattered across it are a baseball Who's Who and bring back nothing but great memories: Mickey Mantle, Roger Maris, Rocky Colavito and Luis Aparicio – some of the greatest baseball players of all time.

I was 11 years old. I woke up that summer morning in 1962, tossed on my cutoffs and headed down to breakfast. My dad was already there. After our "good mornings," we sat at the table and wordlessly slurped our cereal. I cut the baseball cards off the back of my cereal box, and my dad read the sports section.

Suddenly he put down the paper. "How about going to the game today?" he said.

I thought he was joking. First of all, I don't remember if we had ever gone to a game together up until that day. The guy was always working. Second of all, the game at Wrigley Field that afternoon wasn't just any old game. *It was the All-Star Game!* Tickets had been sold out for ever.

"Dad, we'll never get in," I said in my best I-can't-believe-how-dumb-adults-can-be-sometimes whine.

"Let's give it a shot anyways," he said in his always upbeat you-never-know-what-might-happen voice. "Get your jacket and we'll try it."

I was a Chicago Cubs game veteran. My friends and I had already been taking the El to the games for two years. The key to good seats? Buy your ticket, sit in the bleachers early on and then try to sneak into the box seats later when the Andy Frain ushers slacked off a bit.

The technique to getting into the box seats down by the field was fairly easy. Hang out by the concession stand until you saw a guy wearing a suit buy lunch and head back to the boxes. If you could make it look like you were walking with him, like you were his kid, the Andy-Frain-is-a-pain ushers would never snag you. The Cubs were so bad in the early 1960s that, once you made it past the Andy-Frain-has-no-brain, there were always plenty of empty seats.

But not on All-Star day. Wrigley Field was packed solid, standing room only. Somehow, someway my dad got us standing room tickets and we were in!

I love the way Wrigley Field attacks the senses. The smell of the hot dogs and the brilliant green of the grass and the ivy on the wall hit me first. My dad and I ended up sitting on some planks that ran underneath the spiral walkway to the upper deck. My dad boosted me up and handed me our lunch: hot dogs, a Coke and a frosty malt.

Frosty malts were the thing to buy at the ballpark because the vendor, "Fang," was a Wrigley Field institution. The rumor was that he'd been with the team from the beginning and had even helped to hang the famous Wrigley Field vines that cover the brick walls and make the park so special. He had only one tooth – hence his nickname. You could hear him coming two innings before he finally arrived. "Frosthhhy Maaaaaalt!" he would wail. "Getthh yer Froshthhhy Maaalt!"

We bought a scorecard, and I wrote in all the players: Willie Mays, Stan Musial, Mickey Mantle and Roger Maris. I couldn't believe I was really there in person at the All-Star Game.

After the fourth inning, my dad left for a minute. He came back with the red pennant that I am looking at right now and handed it to me. In big, bold letters it reads, "All-Star Game, Chicago, Illinois 1962." The pennant has a green baseball diamond drawn on it and features all of the American League All Stars. I tacked it up over my bed, next to my baseball cards and my Johnny Antonelli autographed glove – and there it stayed until I went away to college. In the dorm, it shared wall space with a Jimmy Hendrix black-light poster, a *Life* magazine cover on Kent State and a montage of fraternity paddles.

After college, I eventually moved away from the lava lamp scene and headed west. That pennant shared wall space with class photos during my school-teaching days and now resides happily on the wall next to Dick Butkus, Sugar Ray Leonard and a photo gallery of a new generation of heroes like Dave

Scott, Mark Allen, Ned Overend and Scott Tinley. There is one more picture on that wall. Below and to the left of my All-Star pennant is a six-foot poster we had made for my dad's 75th birthday three years ago.

For Father's Day this year, I'm flying my dad west for the All-Star Game in San Diego. Hey, big guy . . . this time the hot dogs and frosty malts are on me.

I can't believe it's been 30 years.

Editor's Note: *The 1992 Major League Baseball All-Star Game on July 14 was the 63rd playing of the midsummer classic and was held at what was then called Jack Murphy Stadium (now Qualcomm Stadium) in San Diego, Calif. The American League beat the National League, 13-6, and the MVP was Ken Griffey, Jr.*

BASEBALL CARDS & CLASSIC TRIATHLONS

I knew they were in there somewhere, but I was getting pretty darn close to scrapping the whole project. The month was July, the humidity in the crawl space of my folks' house was stifling and my knees were killing me from scrambling across the concrete. If I wandered mouth first into any more cobwebs, Mickey Mantle, Willie Mays and all those other Hall of Famers playing hide-and-seek tucked away in some ol' shoebox could just go ahead and stay hidden for another 20 years.

The flickering light of my flashlight illuminated any number of crud-en-crusted family heirlooms. Straight ahead were three wooden dad-made toy boxes – my brother's, my sister's and mine. Both of theirs looked brand spanking new. The one that once had BOBBY scripted across the side was missing half the Y, one B and had "Girls are Puke" spray-painted in red across the middle of the O. It was beat to a pulp. Hey, in my mind a toy box with wheels was a rocket ship all fueled up and ready for curb takeoff.

Caught in the glare of my flashlight as I crawled along were a cobweb-encased grass skirt and two wooden paddles with "Cuba" engraved on them. I chuckled out loud and shook my head. My dad's timing was always impeccable. First he bought an Edsel just before that dog went belly up. Then he took my mom on a pleasure cruise to Cuba in 1959, about the same time some guy named Fidel Castro decided to become Cuba's new tour guide. I'm sure Mom looked great in khaki.

Suddenly, out of the corner of my eye, I spotted the treasure. My PF Flyer box filled with what I envisioned as thousands and thousands of dollars of valuable baseball cars. I carefully removed the tape off the box and started sifting through the wreckage. Who woulda thunk it? Baseball cards in mint condition are suddenly worth a ton of money. Mine? They could have been submerged under a ton of melting mints. Warren Sahn's looked like it had been living in my mom's blender since 1965. Willie Mays? He was sporting a pair of very stylish, hand-drawn wire rim glasses.

My heart sank when I picked up Roger Maris' 1962 card. The year after he hit 61 home runs and broke Babe Ruth's record, his card was number one of the set. I don't even want to know what it is worth. My card looks okay except for the blue ink goatee and chest hair that some idiot drew on poor Rog. That same idiot gave Johnny Bench a Fu Manchu mustache and a tattoo (I think he looks pretty darn good).

After recovering from the shock, I realized it really didn't matter. There was no way I would have sold any of my cards anyway. I grew up watching these guys. How could I sell off pieces of my childhood? My ink-covered cards fit right in with my growing endurance sport collection.

My Roger Maris card, beard and all, now shares prime desk space with the results of a Bud Light Triathlon Series event in 1982 in San Diego, California. The first race of the first-ever national triathlon short-course series featured (now) six-time World Ironman Champion Dave Scott, three-time World Ironman Champion Mark Allen, two-time World Ironman Champion Scott Tinley, one-time World Ironman Champions Scott Molina and Kathleen McCartney, plus perpetual masters greats Bill Leach and Gary Hooker.

A number of athletes have used the Bud Light Series as a launching pad to great careers. Molina practically owned the series during the mid-1980s, where he developed his reputation as The Terminator. Mike Pigg made his big breakthrough in the series. So did Kirsten Hanssen, Jan Ripple, Harold Robinson, Colleen Cannon, Joy Hansen, Jimmy Riccitello and Sylvianne and Patricia Puntous.

I met the Puntous sisters for the first time in 1983 at the Bud Light Atlanta event. I was staggering through the 9.3-mile run (the run and swim were longer in those prehistoric days) and breathing like a freight train when these two young ladies ran up next to me. Did I mention that we were going uphill at the time? They probably didn't notice.

Sylvianne was running forward and Patricia was running backward, scanning down the hill to see how far back Julie Leach was. Sylvianne, a five-year multi-sport veteran, turned to me and asked in her best gee-you-look-pathetic French Canadian accent, "Eeeeez theez yer feeerst tri-ath-lon?" Then they disappeared.

One of Andrew Carlson's first triathlons was The San Diego Bud Light in 1989. At the time, he was working parking cars at the Ritz Carlton. He went head-to-head with Scott Molina in that race and finished second but couldn't stay for post-race interviews. He had to get back to work. Three years later, Carlson was a proud member of Team USA and raced in the 1992 World Championships.

The impact of the sport of triathlon has been pretty amazing. And what about the innovations that have come about through triathlon since those early years? Aerodynamic handlebars, lightweight helmets, sunglasses for training and competition, steeper seat tube angles, 26-inch wheels, DayGo clothing (okay, we apologize for that one), bike shoes with Velcro, elastic shoelaces, lace locks, bike fluid replacement systems other than the water bottle, shifters on the handlebars, affordable disc wheels for the age group-competitor, platform pedals and seat-shifting devices.

Furthermore, cross-training has become part of the world vocabulary. Now in the 1990s, runners run less and ride and swim more. Multi-sport fitness is everywhere. Coors Light put on a nationwide duathlon series. Danskin sponsored a national woman's triathlon series that drew over 1,000 women in San Jose, over 900 in New York and 800 in Milwaukee. About 20,000 people annually submit applications to try to get into the Gatorade Ironman, the World Series of the multi-sport world.

Triathlon a fad? I think not. That's why I save all my artifacts from the early days of the sport. Hey, some day all my multi-sport paraphernalia might just be worth something – at least as much as a goateed Roger Maris.

CHAPTER 2

Bob Babbitt at the 1980 Ironman

THE TRI LIFE

WHY TRI?

TRI 101

WHAT I'VE LEARNED

TIPS FROM THE BOTTOM

EVERYONE IN THE POOL

IT'S ALL ABOUT STYLE

THE EQUALIZER

LIFE IN A BUBBLE

MY CAMELOT

IRON JOURNEY

CHAPTER 2 – THE TRI LIFE

"If there is a Camelot in my life, it's a finish line – any finish line."

– Bob Babbitt

WHY TRI?

It's funny. I feel that logic is often the biggest obstacle to accomplishing greatness. How many times over the years have you come up with an idea that excited the heck out of you then eventually backed away from it after staring down every detail?

It's that way when it comes to diving into the wonderful world of triathlon. You're watching television or reading a magazine and you'll spot something on a local or national multi-sport event and you get caught up in the excitement. "I can do that," you'll tell yourself. "I'll be on that starting line next year."

Then the persnickety Mr. Logic sticks his perfectly pleated Dockers in there and reminds you why this is a ridiculous idea: You're too busy, you're too stressed and you're too fat. "These are super athletes," whispers Mr. L. "They've been swimming, cycling and running all their lives, and you could never do that. After you turn that keg into a six pack sometime during the next millennium we can reconvene and re-evaluate."

So you put off taking the leap – again.

The passion of the moment is gone, and Mr. Logic has once again trampled on your dreams.

The too busy logic is pretty easy to get past. No matter how busy you are or how hectic your life is, spending an hour a day working out is going to make you a better parent, partner, employer or employee.

Let's move on to the weight issue. I know that if you are more than a few pounds overweight, your first thought usually isn't, "Hey, I need to go do a triathlon." But you know what? I'm convinced that is exactly what you should be thinking. Mr. Logic would tell you that if you are going to get involved in this nonsense, you should be smart enough to focus on one sport at a time, like running.

I couldn't disagree more. When you are overweight and decide to focus on just running, there is a good chance you are going to end up injured. Newton said it best: W+P=D (Weight plus Pounding equals Disaster).

The other thing that happens when you decide to focus on just running is that your ego can take a tad of a bruising. Moms pushing baby joggers will go by you. It is even more fun when the kid is playing with his SpongeBob Squarepants doll and picking his nose as they scamper by.

The cool part about swimming is that you can get good quickly. You also aren't weight-bearing like you are when running. When I started out in my first masters swimming program, I was in what they call the truck lane with all the other slow guys and gals and a few pregnant women. Within a few weeks, you'll improve enough to move up. Plus, since fat floats, I find it kind of fun to watch the really skinny runner types trying to keep their five percent body fat off the bottom of the pool while I swim by them. Swimming is a great confidence booster. I felt like putting on the cap and gown and inviting my parents out every time I graduated from one lane to another.

Cycling, for the most part, doesn't discriminate either. If you are riding the flat roads along the coast or taking an indoor cycling class, you can cruise along with anyone – no matter how fit they are. When the climbs come, you'll definitely suffer. I think it was Albert Einstein who came up with the mass of the ass theory. On the downhills, though, you will be like King Kong and make everyone pay.

As you begin to reshape your body through swimming and cycling, you can start to add in some running. Walking and running is a good way to get into it. Before you know it, you'll be running two to four miles at a clip. More importantly, you'll stay injury free, and you'll actually enjoy running. After you have built up a swim, bike and run base, that's the time to think about bumping up your running mileage and maybe joining a marathon training program.

I wrote a book with a wonderful woman named Judy Molnar a few years back called *You Don't Have to Be Thin to Win*. Molnar had been a volleyball player in high school and college but gained a ton of weight after entering the workplace. (Hey, it's not hard when your first media client is a donut shop.)

One day, Molnar was at the doctor's office getting a physical when she took a gander at her chart while the doctor was out of the room. The words 'morbidly obese' jumpstarted her transition. She got into the pool, started riding a bike, eventually lost 130 pounds and completed an Ironman triathlon.

She started with short triathlons that served as three- and six-month goals. As she moved up in distance, she ended up being a guest on the *Rosie O'Donnell Show* to talk about her journey. O'Donnell liked the message so much that after Molnar finished the Ironman, O'Donnell hired her to run the Chub Club that ended up with over 300,000 members.

Now, believe it or not, Molnar actually works for the Ironman, running the IronGirl division of the company.

Molnar told Mr. Logic to shove off and started swimming, cycling and running her way to a dream come true. It all starts with taking that first step.

Why tri? There is absolutely no reason not to.

TRI 101

A lot of tri-words we might take for granted could be confusing for newbies, so here's my updated triathlon vocabulary list. Study up! The test will be Tuesday.

Anaerobic: To go very fast. To hurt lots and lots. To breathe heavier than a 1-900 caller.

Getting "babied": There is nothing worse than mom or dad going by you pushing a baby jogger while Junior dozes with binky, blanket and Barney. Ouch!

Body marking: At each event, your race number will be put on your arms and your age on your calf with a magic marker. Some triathletes have started to add personal info. Some as a warning – divorced with way too much baggage; or some as an enticement – single with a really, really large trust fund. Both are much appreciated.

Bonk: Reaching the point in your race or workout where the body just refuses to go anymore. See *Anaerobic* . . . then go just a little bit harder.

Getting "chicked": Get used to it, guys, and just face the music. Tri gals are tougher, faster and fitter. Whether it's your 12-year-old neighbor or your best friend's granny, women love to run you down.

Cookie: Someone who falls apart easily. As in, "When I went by him on the bike, he crumbled like a cookie."

Cramp: Your first one hits at the start. The fun part is stereo cramps, when both hamstrings seize up during the run. Then you stagger across the finish with that cool Frankenstein-like stiff-legged look while your friends point and laugh.

Drafting: Sitting behind someone and letting them break the wind – or water – for you. Legal in the swim (see *Facial*) and the run. Very illegal and very much frowned upon on the bike (see Bernie Madoff, Al Capone *or Mass Murderer*).

Extinct: Something that has not survived the test of time. Dinosaurs are extinct. Eight-tracks are extinct. The Seat Shifter and 26-inch wheels are extinct. For us older triathletes, sub-eight-minute miles are extinct.

Facial: What you get if you draft behind someone's feet in the swim for too long. As in, "I didn't think that dude knew I was there. Then he slowed down and gave me a two-footed facial."

Iliotibial band: A slab of muscle on the outside of your thigh. Unless you're a triathlete, you'd never know you had one. If you're a triathlete, they ache all the time, and you become very aware that you have two.

Ironman: The goal, the Holy Grail, for many a triathlete. You'll hate the first 140 miles. You'll never forget that last six-tenths.

Jellyroll: The flabby thing that won't go away. It wraps around your waist and jiggles every time you run. The Jellyroll helps differentiate the haves from the have-nots. The pros have not. You have.

Nutrition: Something you'll be very concerned about – until after the race. Then it's Big Macs, Whoppers, fries, onion rings and secret sauce for everyone!

Overdraft: A nickname for someone notorious for passing you early and then falling apart later on. "He'll/She'll come back to me like a bad check," you'll say to yourself.

Tinkle: In a duathlon or a running event, something you do in a bush, behind a tree or in a port-a-potty before the race. In triathlon, something you do in your own personal port-a-potty: your wetsuit.

UFO: Unidentified Flying Object. Anything moving faster than you either on a bike or on foot. As in, "That guy went by me like a UFO."

X-wife, x-husband, x-girlfriend, x-boyfriend: If A = a lot of time submerged in the water, B = a lot of time on the bike and C = a lot of time running, then A+B+C=X.

Zambia: One of the few countries Ironman doesn't have an event in – yet.

WHAT I'VE LEARNED

You'd think that after spending the better part of the past 35 years in this sport I would have learned it all by now. Not even close. Every single day I'm lucky to learn even more about the best sport on the planet. Some lessons I've learned so far:

Keep the change. When you complete an Ironman event and your time is somewhere between 11:30 and 11:59, never tell people your actual time. Nope. If someone asks your time, say, "I went 11 and change." Definitely more impressive than 11:59:59. At the end of the day, does it really matter how much change we're talking about? I didn't think so.

Experts are great, but becoming an expert on you is even better. Chris McCormack always had problems in the Kona heat during his early days of racing Hawaii. He worked with physiologists and nutritionists to figure out the best ways for a "bigger" guy like him to deal with the heat and to fuel up during the race. In 2005, as he was falling further off the pace on the way out to the bike turnaround in Hawi, 1996 Ironman World Champion Thomas Hellriegel passed him, could tell he was struggling and suggested that Macca drink some Coke. "I was told to never drink Coke in a race by the nutritionists," Macca says. "I was pretty frustrated and desperate at that point of the race, so I drank a Coke and it was like jet fuel." McCormack had his best Kona that day up until that point, ran 2:49 off the bike and finished sixth, his first time in the top 10. He learned the hard way that, no matter what the experts say, for him a little carbonated syrup plus caffeine can actually be a good thing.

$300 is $300. I was racing the Chicago Triathlon one year, and as I passed a guy on the bike – which, by the way, is about as rare as a solar eclipse – I noticed he had the sleeves of his wetsuit tied around his neck and the rest of the suit was flapping behind him like a huge rubber-coated kite. "Why do you have your wetsuit with you?" I asked. He looked at me like I was nuts. "What? I just paid $300 for this thing, and I'm supposed to take it off and leave it in a parking lot?"

Never run by an aid station. Take this to the bank. As soon as you feel like you're in control during a race, you're not. Grab something, anything, at every aid station, or you're guaranteed to regret it. You might not suffer the consequences right this minute, but you will definitely pay the price for not taking a gel, water, salt, electrolyte drink, pretzels or gummy bears.

Remember your priorities. When we are living our daily lives, we are concerned and have to deal with money, emails, employees, employers, dressing nice, family, friends and so much more. When we race, the most important things in our life for those few hours become our bike, watch, wetsuit, goggles, running shoes and that oh-so-refreshing ice-cold sponge. At the end of the day, does anything else really matter?

Prison weapons are good. "Hey Babbitt," a fellow 60-to-death age grouper yelled at me as he passed me during a race this summer, "that bike is from the last CENTURY!" I was about to say something back to him when I realized how right he was, that I bought my bike back in 1998. The good news? Not long after that I upgraded to a Specialized Shiv, which I love. The message? If a bike is named after a prison instrument like a Shiv or a Shank, it's probably pretty damn fast.

TIPS FROM THE BOTTOM

Most magazines tend to showcase items like "tips from the top" for their how-to sections. It makes sense. If you're reading a martial arts, scuba diving, running or knitting magazine, who wants to take advice from the always-limping 12-minute miler, the scuba diver with twin squid stuck in his mask, the martial arts professional nicknamed "Oops!" or the knitting "expert" whose book is titled *Knit Like S**t?*

After years of hanging out in transition areas, I have some tips that, while they won't make you faster, can make your race experience a tad more enjoyable:

Parking. Most events have limited parking. Since I don't sleep well the night before a race because I'm so nervous about sleeping through multiple alarms, I get up way early, grab my pillow and blanket and beat the race director to the site, which will be my only win of the day. My theory: Being relaxed is better than having to park farther from the start than the actual distance of the race.

Now that I'm in the best parking spot, I get the heated seat going, take a nap and check out a little sports radio. Then I hit the pristine, yet-to be-used port-a-potties, pump up my tires and rack my bike. I'm awake, relaxed and ready to go. Plus I'm parked 10 feet from transition, so my exit strategy is golden.

Racking. In life, I always err on the side of comfort. When I go into transition, I would much rather grab an end spot even though it's not considered the fastest place to be. The reality? I don't care. If I'm at the wall end of the rack, I can grab lots of space, not be in anyone's way and spread out. When I get out of the water and need to get my wetsuit off and bike shoes on, there's nothing better. The wall is awesome. It's tough to get your balance after the swim, so something solid can be huge. When you get to be my age, you are always looking for something – or someone – to lean on.

Warming up. This is a big issue for folks who don't like the cold. I learned this lesson the hard way. Back before wave starts, a race would advertise a 7 a.m. kick-off. Most times the races didn't start until 7:20. Big problem.

I'd be at the water's edge and my foot thermometer was telling me that the water was sub-60. I'd warm up before the start, but then the race would be delayed 20 minutes. I'd be shivering with blue lips and chattering teeth more often than I care to remember from jumping into a cold body of water before wetsuits were commonly worn. It was a personalized invitation to the Shrinkage Hotel.

My suggestion is to never to warm up before the actual start unless you happen to be in the first wave. I make sure the event starts on time. Then, since I'm in the 60-to-death category, I wait until the wave in front of mine takes off before warming up. That gives me five solid minutes to acclimate and remind my body what swimming actually feels like.

At the end of the day, my race day tips will probably not make you faster.

They will, however, help keep you warm, comfy and happy. What could be better than that?

EVERYONE IN THE POOL

I've been a huge proponent of the reverse triathlon – 3.1-mile run, 10-mile bike and 150-yard swim in a pool – for at least 15 years.

Why? Simple. The barrier to trying a tri – the greatest sport on the planet in my opinion – is the swim. If you get tired while running or cycling you can sit down, catch your breath, walk a bit and relax. But if you get tired during the swim what can you do? People panic and wonder how the heck they are going to get back to shore. Plus, from a newbie's perspective, an open-water swim is a virtual minefield. It's usually barely light at the start, the water is dark and probably cold, the current might drag you to Guatemala, you could get swatted in the head by some guy who cracks walnuts with his forearms just for fun and yeah, I did see *Jaws* and big gray things with large teeth really scare the living hell out of me.

But in a reverse triathlon, the 5K warms you up, and most anyone can run or walk that far. The bike ride is usually two mellow five-mile loops, and anyone can do that – even on a 61-pound Sears cruiser with a bell and tassels. After dismounting the bike, you'll grab your goggles, jog to the 80-degree, crystal-clear pool, serpentine your way across using the crawl, sidestroke, backstroke, breast stroke or even the dog paddle. There are lifeguards, walls to hang on to, no fish, no seaweed and, like the run and the bike, anyone can do it.

I believe that if the 150-yard swim were removed from the event, the numbers would drop from the 1,200 who were at the last Tinsel Tri in December to half that. Why? Because triathlon is sexy and everyone wants to do one so they can join the hippest club around.

How do I know? Flash back three years ago. We had just finished the Tinsel Tri in Hemet, California. The guy next to me at the awards was in board shorts and no shirt, and he had a bike with high bars and a belly no doubt envied by sumo wrestlers.

The announcer declared that the Ironman would be airing that afternoon and that we should tune in.

Sumo guy's wife was standing right next to him and looked perplexed. "Honey," she asked, "what's the Ironman?"

"Same thing I just did," insisted Mr. 3-mile run, 10-mile bike and 150-yard swim in a pool. "Just a little longer."

If Ironman World Champion Chris McCormack had been strolling by at that exact moment, the guy who just did an event totaling 13 miles would have felt right at home, considering himself a kindred spirit to a guy who just raced 140.6 miles in the heat and wind of the Kona coast.

But you know what? Sumo boy was spot on. At the end of the day, the order and distance don't really matter. If it takes less than an hour or more than 16, if you swim, bike and run and finish what you start, you're a triathlete.

What could be better than that?

IT'S ALL ABOUT STYLE

Okay, so it's not the best look in the world. But, hey, the year was 1980, there were only 108 of us lined up for the swim start in Waikiki and there really wasn't any dress code for this unknown event called the Ironman. Heck, Dave Scott won the race, and he was wearing a cotton tank top and tube socks. He also had his folks follow him in a rented station wagon with a spare bike strapped down to the top of the car. Compared to this guy, I was positively GQ.

So let's go through my Ironman outfit piece by piece:

Bike. It was a Centurion, I think. I bought it at a police auction for $75 three weeks before the race. It had been in a minor fire – the translation of "minor fire" means you yourself did not become a briquette in it. Good looking, don't you think? Of course I made some minor alterations to make it a tad more aerodynamic. We've got the padded handlebars, the fuzzy raccoon seat cover, the Radio Shack radio bungee-corded to said handlebars to keep the 112 miles from being obnoxiously dull, the panniers and the sleeping bag. *The what?* Let me explain. When I first came to Oahu, I thought you did the event in two days: swim 2.4 miles, ride 56 miles, camp out, get up in the morning, ride 56 miles then run the marathon. This do-it-all-in-one-day stuff totally took me by surprise.

Kickstand. You never know when you've got to get off your bike and stretch your legs. I certainly wasn't going to lay my prize possession down on the ground and scratch the already charred paint.

Reflectors. Can you say riding in the dark? I certainly thought I might be.

Solid rubber tires. Some of us are, shall we say, mechanically challenged. I really had no idea how to change a tire so I simply had solid rubber tires put on the bike. No need to carry extra tires. So what if it felt like you were riding a jackhammer? I knew I'd never have to stop for a flat. Plus, these puppies had the shelf life of Velveeta, a Hostess Twinkie or Dick Clark. They are simply nuclear-attack proof. Sort of like the black box on a plane. I want to sit by that thing when I fly. When the plane disintegrates into millions of microscopic particles, they always find the black box totally intact. My tires were like that.

The beard and afro. I looked like Che Guevara on the lamb and, yes, I could store food for months in there. I don't think the beard was that aerodynamic in the water. Can you say very large sponge? But when I first flew to Oahu, it certainly was worth a few laughs. See, Gordon Haller won the Ironman in 1978, the first-ever champion. He had a big beard. I was on the plane in 1980 from San Diego to Honolulu along with a bunch of Navy SEALs going to do their first Ironman as well. They see the beard and think I'm Gordon Haller, former Ironman champion. They see the bike you are looking at roll off the plane – this is before bike boxes – and think this is the bike that won the Ironman. They were checking my stead out like it was Lance Armstrong's bike from the Tour de France. Hmmmm . . . fuzzy raccoon seat cover . . . radio . . . solid rubber tires . . . this Gordon Haller guy must know something we don't. That visual still makes me laugh.

Hat. It was a silly little cycling cap with the brim turned up like it's supposed to be, right? When my roommate, Ned Overend, and I first decided to do this Ironman thing, we tried cycling in our rock-climbing helmets, which had no holes for ventilation. After 10 miles, the heat was so overwhelming we thought our melons were going to explode. Hence, the move to the funny-looking cycling cap.

Long-sleeve cotton shirt. Always good in the islands. You never know when the temperature might plummet to a brisk 87 degrees and you certainly want to be prepared. I sewed pockets on the back of the long-sleeve shirt and, even though I had a support crew driving a convertible Fiat with most of my gear in it, I still had enough Hawaiian Sweet Bread in my back pocket to feed Guatemala. To supplement the Hawaiian Sweet Bread, my crew supplied me with all the race-day nutrition I really needed: Big Mac, fries and a Coke at mile 25 – plus a bitchin' snow cone at mile 80.

Khaki bike shorts with pockets. Yep . . . they had pockets and a chamois to keep all of my moving parts happy. I didn't really know about the bun-hugger bike shorts yet and, quite frankly, I think this was a better look anyway. Hey . . . I'm the only Ironman finisher in history to wear a leather belt during the bike ride. People sometimes wonder why I got inducted into the Ironman Hall of Fame. Maybe it had something to do with my particular sense of style.

Race number 3. Did the race folks mistake me for Gordon Haller as well? Was I seeded? Not quite. Did I send my $10 entry fee in really early? That's my guess. Whenever someone asks about my best finish in Hawaii, I tell them about 1980. I was 55th overall at the Ironman Triathlon World Championship. Who needs to know that there were only 108 starters? We'll keep that between us as our little secret. SHHHH!

The bottom line. My tube socks came up to the knees, just like my homeboy Dave Scott. My shoes were Jack Purcell tennis shoes, and we used cages on the pedals. To be honest, I never realized that you were supposed to reach down and actually tighten the straps of the cages on your shoes. I thought that putting your feet into the cages somehow magically made you one with the pedals. My bad.

THE EQUALIZER

It happens all the time. We see that really cool wetsuit with the built-in six-pack abs or the hot new tri bike that weighs less than a foot-long tuna melt from Subway and immediately chuckle and keep on walking. So why do age-groupers like us have problems digging into our wallets every once in a while and anteing up for new equipment? It's simple, really: We feel we aren't worthy.

In our minds, top pros deserve the top equipment. Hey, we're only lowly age-groupers. We deserve our bike that is 26 pounds of solid steel and a used wetsuit from that sumo wrestler down the street. Anything better, in our warped minds, would be way beyond our tri status.

I'm here to tell you that this attitude should be as extinct as the Skid Lid, Seat Shifter and the Tri 101 Series. Rather than deprive yourself of the best, you should be *rewarding* yourself with anything that can make you even a pinch faster. We deserve the very best equipment because the cards are already stacked against us:

- On race day, the pros, with their $5,000, 17-pound aerodynamic bullet machines, get to rack their bikes 5 feet from the water's edge. We rack ours in Bangor, Maine.

- The pro field is usually minimal, maybe 20 genetic freaks total. They have plenty of open water. Our wave starts are so crowded we end up in hand-to-hand combat for most of the swim with chowderheads taking turns playing the bongos on our rubber-covered noggin – not fun.

- The pros get to go off first. That way they don't have to weave through 1,000 other cyclists or deal with those minor annoyances – also known as heat and wind – that we live with every race.

- Of course the top guys and gals run fast. They are 3 percent body fat. Most of us were well north of 14 percent at birth.

- While you are up at 5 a.m. to ride the trainer in the living room before heading out for a run and a swim before heading off to work, the pros are sleeping in till 9 and filling their days with swimming, napping, getting a massage, cycling, napping some more while squeezing in some quality Starbucks latté time. You, of course, have to dress up in business attire for your 10-hour workday and deal with people who don't get your passion for triathlon and question the constant nasal drip and permanent goggle marks that come with the tri territory.

Back in the early 1990s, I too believed that I was not worthy. Then I had a wake-up call. I was flying to Tahiti for a triathlon and Kenny Souza, the very best duathlete in the world at the time, loaned me his bike bag for the trip. When I came by his house to pick it up, he had a surprise for me. Inside the bike bag was his personalized Nishiki Altron. During the Tahiti race, for the first time in my life, I rode a bike that was actually a rocket ship in disguise. Instead of holding firm at 19 miles per hour on my solid steel dinosaur, the Kenny Souza bike, with the same effort from me, was humming along at a sweet 22.

That, my friends, is why you deserve the very best. We need great equipment much more than the fast guys and gals just to level the playing field. They are younger, faster, leaner, stronger and have a maximum heart rate that would make a hummingbird jealous.

So get out there and buy yourself the very best. And try to stifle that laugh as you fly by fellow age-groupers who used to own you.

LIFE IN A BUBBLE

It's my first race of the season, and I'm in the zone. I finish the swim and, even though I never would've passed the walk-a-straight-line DUI test after being immersed in mid-50-degree water, I somehow manage to make my way through transition, shivering the whole time. After trying to stay upright on one leg while strapping my bike shoes to those blocks of ice hanging off the end of each leg, I eventually mount up and head off.

Throughout the ride, I was actually able to pass people. The fact that they were still wearing their wetsuits, riding $69 mountain bikes and wearing their helmets backward makes absolutely no difference to me. Passing is passing, right? What they ride, how old they are and how long they have been in the sport means nothing. The key for me when it comes to racing is to put myself in what I call my "never a bad day bubble" – which is the way I love to race.

There are times on race day when you can get upset and everything is a big deal. You can either complain about the situation or simply disavow any knowledge of it. I, for one, choose to look the other way and ignore anything that even resembles reality.

Negative Thought (NT): The swim is long and the lake is really choppy.
Never a Bad Day Bubble (NABDB): Good. How often do you get to get to swim in a blender – that'll definitely be something fun to chat about in the beer garden.

NT: Our 60-to-death age group goes off after everyone else – what a bummer!
NABDB: Going off later is awesome. We're not starting in the dark, the sun is out, there is no port-a-potty line, we can pass younger folks in the water, and it's pretty darn easy to find my bike in the racks.

NT: I'm not even to the turnaround of the swim yet!
NABDB: I'm almost halfway to the turnaround buoy, and when I get there I'm halfway back to the beach. Sweet!

NT: Man, it is windy out here today.
NABDB: Wind is my friend. Tough days suit tough people.

NT: Where the hell is that next aid station?
NABDB: This is awesome. It's not racing; it's a catered workout. People volunteer their time to hand us food and drink? How cool is that?

NT: The fast people keep passing me on the bike.
NABDB: There is no "R" drawn on their calf, but I know everyone who passes me must be on a relay team. Relay people *should* be passing me.

NT: My legs feel really heavy, and I'm running like a 90-year-old.
NABDB: I finally passed that 90-year-old. I bet she was an Olympian back in the day.

NT: It's lonely out here. I haven't seen anyone in forever.
NABDB: How often do I get to spend time with just me and not have to deal with e-mails, text messages or calls?

NT: It's so hot!
NABDB: I wonder who came up with the idea of the cold sponge? It just might be the world's greatest invention.

NT: Crap, I'm 12th in my age group, and there were only 14 of us.
NABDB: Everyone in the race gets a medal – I love that! If it weren't for slow guys like me getting our butts kicked, how would fast people know they were fast? The world needs us!

MY CAMELOT

I love racing. There is nothing better in the whole wide world. Some people I know get stressed out just thinking about race morning. But for me, if it's a Saturday or Sunday and there are no numbers scrawled on my legs and arms, I get the shakes. Here is why racing is a heck of a lot more fun than training:

- Swag is the key. Every time you race you get a goodie bag, a t-shirt and a finisher's medal. Maybe even a cookie. When you train? All you get is sore.

- It doesn't matter if you're not very good. Actually, being slow is important. Otherwise, how would the fast guys and gals ever know how awesome they are? They have to be way in front of *somebody* to feel good about themselves and impress the world. That's where people like me come in. You're welcome, fast guys.

- People cheer for you no matter how crappy you're doing. And they'll always smile and say something awesome like "You're almost there," even though you never are. I love that.

- New races equal new roads and new trails. In local races you get acquainted with parts of your neighborhood that you didn't even know existed.

- You will always have someone to chat with during the run and bike, which at the end of the day is why we do this stuff anyway. Make new friends, tell jokes. There are lots of great folks to hang out with, and I don't even have to pay them or buy them breakfast to spend time with me!

- Racing allows you to create your own reality. In my mind, nobody ever passes me on race day. I just decide beforehand that anyone who passes is actually part of a relay team, even if they're not. For some of us, denial is a good thing.

- Races usually start early and, if they are short triathlons, you can actually be done and in the beer garden before most of your friends and family are awake. 9 a.m. is the ultimate time to kick off happy hour.

If there is a Camelot in my life, it's a finish line – any finish line. The sponsors are happy, the race directors are happy, the volunteers are happy, the announcers are happy and, of course, the athletes are ecstatic. Everyone is cheering, and there is a feeling of accomplishment that hangs in the air no matter how long or tough the race. Then you get to savor the rest of the day and that great finish-line-induced adrenaline high. Of course, we all know that this amazing feeling won't last forever – which is why you need to hurry home and figure out where you'll be racing next weekend.

IRON JOURNEY

There's one room in my house that's a shrine to the sport of triathlon. Protected in plastic is the 1979 *Sports Illustrated* that showcased Ironman and put us on the map. Since I have been fortunate enough to be at every Ironman in Hawaii since 1980, I have a copy of every Ironman program and the Hawaiian newspaper post-race coverage. A shriveled lei from one of my finishes hangs with medals and photos. The athletic résumés that the 108 of us filled out prior to the 1980 race are there.

John Howard, who gave the Ironman credibility just by showing up, had a résumé that included a Pan American Games Gold Medal, three Olympic teams and the honor of being named *Competitive Cycling Magazine's* Cyclist of the Decade for the 1970s.

Dave McGillivray, who would become the race director of the Boston Marathon, mentioned in his that he had run more than 3,000 miles across the United States to raise money for charity and averaged more than 50 miles a day.

Dave Scott's was fairly understated. He insisted that he had a swimming and water polo background, but not much else. Next to Scott's résumé I have a photo of him on his way to winning that 1980 Ironman. Obviously already fashion-conscious, he is on the bike sporting a floppy tank top, no helmet and way-ahead-of-his-time compression socks that stretch almost to his knees. If you look at the photo closely, you can spot a station wagon behind him with a spare bike bungee-corded to the top. Yep, that was Scott's mom and dad, Verne and Dot, making sure their boy was taken care of. Who would have figured back in the day that their boy would become The Man when it came to the Ironman?

On one shelf is a red radio. The two of us shared a cool 112-mile bike ride back in 1980. It was bungee-corded to the padded handlebars of my $75 fire-damaged police auction bike, which also had a fuzzy raccoon seat cover and solid rubber tires, because I couldn't change a flat, plus panniers holding my sleeping bag and tent. Since I thought Ironman was a two-day event (swim 2.4 miles and ride 56 miles on day one and then ride 56 miles and run 26.2 on day two), it made sense to carry a portable hotel room, right?

When I emerged from Ala Moana Channel, I put on my long-sleeve shirt along with khaki shorts and belt, mounted up and headed off on the second part of my Ironman adventure. Riding through Waikiki, I turned on my radio and started to enjoy a day that I will never forget.

My crew gave me a Big Mac, fries and a Coke about 25 miles into the ride, a root beer snow cone at mile 80 then a 45-minute massage between the bike and the run – which means I probably have one of the longest Ironman bike-to-run transitions ever.

The marathon was more of a walk and shuffle than a run, but it didn't matter. By that time, I had already surprised myself. I had no idea that I could complete this unbelievable event all in one day. So when I did, I felt like I now had this business card in my pocket for the rest of my life that let me know I could accomplish anything I set my mind to – whether it was in business, sport or life.

My Ironman Hall of Fame trophy.

Wandering through the room makes me realize just how far the sport – and I – have come over the past 30 years.

And every artifact in there reminds me how awesome the journey has been.

The Running Elvi

PRICELESS NUGGETS

TIDBITS TO LIVE BY

SAVOR THE LITTLE THINGS

MY THOUGHTS ON "TRAINING"

WHY IT'S GOOD TO BE BAD

TAKING IT FROM SPORTS

BABBITTVILLE

CHAPTER 3 – PRICELESS NUGGETS

"Don't think of these events as 'races.' That can totally scare you off. They are just 'catered workouts.' As you run mindlessly along, someone will hand you something to eat and drink. Does that happen when you go for a run from your house? Hardly."

– Bob Babbitt

TIDBITS TO LIVE BY

It hit me the other day: Some of the most important lessons we learn in life don't necessarily come from the classroom or from the boardroom. Nope. I think most of the wisdom I have gleamed on to comes from the different events I have found myself at over the years. Not only are endurance sports great in terms of fitness, but after nearly 30 years of hanging around finish lines in places as diverse as Switzerland, Borneo, Tahiti, Guatemala, El Salvador, Kona, Chicago, Los Angeles and Mission Bay, there are certain tidbits that I use every day of my life.

The simplest things can be the best gifts. When it's 100 degrees out and you feel like the sauna has been turned up to full blast, something as simple as an ice cube or a cold sponge can become the greatest gift on earth.

No matter how prepared you are, you're not. You get up for an event at 4 a.m. and arrive at the race site two hours early. You leisurely set up your transition area and are as calm as calm can be. But 20 minutes before your wave is ready to go, you hear what sounds like a gunshot and you just know it's your tire that blew. Or you look down and realize that you left your timing chip in the car. You can either panic and feel sorry for yourself or simply take care of the problem and move on.

Make the best of the moment. I learned this from six-time Ironman World Champion Mark Allen. He was sick as a dog the morning of the Nice Triathlon in France, an event that he had already won nine times in a row. He really wasn't sure if he could even start the race. Knowing that he wouldn't be anywhere near 100 percent, Allen made the decision that he would race but that he would change his expectations. Since he felt he was functioning at 50 or 60 percent of his potential, he would try to get 100 percent out of whatever it was he had that day and be happy with the effort. He ended up coming from behind and winning his 10th – and last – Nice Triathlon title. Message: There will be days where you're not 100 percent, so get 100 percent out of whatever you happen to have that day and be happy with the effort.

Everyone hurts. So you're a multimillionaire, an eye surgeon, a janitor or a high school dropout. Out on the course in a singlet and shorts, everyone is the same. You swim, you ride, you run or you do all three on the same day. The endurance gods are equal opportunity destroyers – everyone hurts. It doesn't matter if you are there to win or just to finish. At the end of the day, we're all just a bunch of geeks with really weird tan lines.

Don't underestimate anyone. Tom Sullivan is a blind entertainer who has sung the national anthem at the Super Bowl, has been a contributor to *Good Morning America* and had a movie made of his life called *If You Could See What I Hear.* He is also my tandem triathlon partner. We were in Boulder, Colorado one summer at an Ironman Training Camp when we got lost out in the middle of nowhere. We had started out with the group on a 75-mile bike ride but got lost. (Did I mention that I am directionally challenged and have trouble just finding my car in the parking lot?) I was starting to panic, as absolutely nothing looked familiar. From behind me, I heard this calm voice of reason. "Bob," said Sullivan, "in about a quarter mile there will be a gravel road on your left. Take that and it will lead back to the main road." Blind? I don't think so.

Don't underestimate anyone (part two). After our first-ever triathlon together, Sullivan and I were rehashing the events of the day at a local eatery. Before we became high tech, our tandem weighed in at 70 pounds and had fuzzy raccoon seat covers and a pink flamingo mounted on the front. I was famished and finished my food before Sullivan. His fries looked great and the guy is blind, right? So I snuck more than a few. As we continued to chat, I asked him about growing up blind and what was the worst part of that experience. "The worst part?" he smiled. "Dealing with jerks who stole my fries."

You deserve the best especially if you're not the best. In the beginning, I used to think that only the best athletes should be using high-priced running shoes, great wetsuits, disc wheels, racing flats and titanium components. It took years for me to realize that it's not a matter of deserving; it's a matter of who needs it the most. It's reality. Hey, the fast guys and gals park their bikes at the water's edge. A lot of us more "mature" athletes need to take a cab from the swim finish to where our bikes are parked in the transition area. We definitely need the fast stuff more than the fast guys do.

Break everything in life down into small chunks. When you were a kid, your dad cut your food into little bite-size portions that you could handle. When I first started doing marathons and the Ironman, I learned to cut these longer events into small bite-size chunks that I could handle. When you think of the whole enchilada, the task seems overwhelming. But when you take 26.2 miles of running or 140.6 miles of a triathlon and break it down, life is so much easier.

One year, a few of us were hurting big time in the Ironman marathon. We invented something we called the Telephone Pole Marathon to stay motivated. We ran to one telephone pole and then walked to the next. Our group grew to about 15. We made the best of what could have been a depressing situation. The same thing transfers to to that pile of work on your desk. One step at a time and only visualize the immediate pole . . . I mean goal.

You never know. This is the way Dave Scott went into the 1989 Japan Ironman. His wife was due to have their first child any minute. His knee was hurting. He had gotten lost two days before the race and rode five hours in what was supposed to be a short tune-up ride. He thought there was a good chance he couldn't even finish the race, so the night before he called the airline to change to an earlier flight since he was pretty sure he'd be dropping out. He pumped his tires up to 185 pounds and left his spare tire and frame pump behind. Scott took the lead 100 meters into the swim and went on to set the record for the Ironman distance at the time with an 8:01. When he went to pick up his bike the next day, he had a flat tire. Feeling lousy about the planning for a presentation? Thinking of canceling the appointment? Think of Dave Scott. You never know.

SAVOR THE LITTLE THINGS

I am lightheaded, floating on air somewhere between Squaw Valley and Auburn, California. Vaseline has proven useless. The blisters between my toes are bloody and rubbed Howard Stern raw. The water bottles attached to my waistbelt rattle and gurgle with each and every stride. A leak in one causes a constant spittle that oozes out of the top and drips from calf to ankle to trail.

My field of vision – my vision of life – has narrowed significantly in this, my third consecutive 25-mile running day. Yellow ribbons are my only link to the dusty trail, and they are up high, attached to overhanging tree limbs. Danger is down low, where ankle-snapping rocks and hidden tree roots lurk in the shadows. I try to balance my vision, to look high for ribbons and low for obstacles at the same time so as not to miss a turn. My synapses are at the ready and adrenaline is on call, standing at attention.

The real world simply does not exist in my mind at this point. Life is all too simple. Run a few strides, spot a ribbon, scan for danger and slurp some fluid.

Repeat.

The idea was to give some of the less ambitious in town (namely me) the chance to run the Western States 100 with a touch of sanity thrown in. Instead of doing the deed in 24 hours or less, instead of enrolling in Sleep Deprivation University, we invitees of the American Medical Joggers Association would camp out at night and have all of four days to finish the course.

Even with the luxuries of a tent and sleeping bag, you still have to navigate 100 miles of trails in four days, the only 100-mile training week of my seriously under-trained life. Work and cars and friends are replaced with a new focal point. The trail that stretches out to eternity in front of me is my only concern.

I have made the world's most inexcusable mistake numerous times already. Zoning out on the beauty around me or thinking about old Three Stooges reruns for what seems like only a few nanoseconds, I fail to note one of the yellow ribbons that mark the course. Finally realizing my mistake, I find myself far off course and forced to backtrack.

Face it. The workout is long enough, thank you. There is nothing more aggravating – or worthless – than running 105 miles.

Halfway through day three, a ridiculous number of miles into our journey, my running partner and I are suddenly at the end of the trail. The dirt road connects to something we barely recognize. It's called a street. On this "street" are people – lots of sleeping in, omelet-eating, football-watching, Big Mac-devouring normal people. They are lined up 10-deep in front of perfectly manicured lawns and white picket fences.

Big trucks pulling big trees are heading down what looks like Main Street. What's all the commotion?

The two of us are coated from head to toe with trail dust. Two potential mass murderers, the words tattooed on our puny forearms. We look like two wackos stumbling out of the woods, and the citizens of Foresthill obviously agree.

After the flatbed lumber trucks come troops of Cub Scouts and Boy Scouts. As we walk toward downtown and parents scurry to save their children, it finally hits us. We were so out of touch, so into our own little running world, we forgot that this was the Fourth of July! Small children are up on their daddies' shoulders waving American flags while we (dusty degenerates in bloody running shoes) are wandering the streets. What could be more festive?

Fortunately, I prepare for any eventuality. I had put a five-dollar bill in my pack about a month before and forgot about it. We find a Mr. Frosty shop in downtown Foresthill, and I treat us both to chocolate milkshakes.

We grab a seat in the sun, stretch our legs out and sit back to watch the scouts and the rest of the parade meander by. Some time later, we go searching for and find our trail, and finish up our third and fourth days of almost-marathon running.

It's the little things in life that stand out. Ever been in a long, hot bike race and get handed a really cold sponge? Or how about an ice cube at mile 20 of a marathon? You put it in your mouth and roll it around with your tongue. It's like the best gift you have ever received!

Coming into Foresthill on a fluke and getting to see a small-town American Fourth of July celebration was like that.

I've searched worldwide to find a chocolate milkshake that tastes anywhere near as good as that one, but I don't think it will happen. The shake still tastes so good because that memory still tastes so good.

MY THOUGHTS ON "TRAINING"

First of all, don't be misled. When it comes to training for and running a marathon, I really have no clue what I am doing. Looking to me for training advice is like calling up Mike Tyson for investment help. Remember, I'm the guy who, when I had a facial explosion at the age of 12, believed his older brother when he told me to look under my pillow for a quarter from the zit fairy. Bright is not really one of my best attributes.

Yes, I have finished a ton of marathons, but many have been either staggering through the lava fields of Kona in the 1980s at the end of the Ironman or, in the past decade, dressed for success in a full-length sweat and Gatorade-stained white Lycra Elvis outfit or as a huge foam rubber Jamba Juice banana. Okay, I've also hiked my way over, around and through at least 15 Catalina Marathons. But most of those have been with a camera in tow and enough energy gels in my pockets to feed the entire nation of Guatemala. In one, I actually wore a red shirt and tried to pose for a photo with a pawing-at-the-ground-I'd-really-like-to-maim-this-loser buffalo.

Again, not quite a nominee for the Bright Hall of Fame.

But I feel that it is necessary to offer a little point/counterpoint to my buddy, TJ Murphy, who plans out specific training programs. They are concise, to the point and, if you follow them, you are guaranteed an enjoyable and healthy racing experience.

But is that really what you are looking for? Come on... I know you are out there. Who is with me on this? The word *training* just doesn't sound like that much fun to me. If that sounds like fun to you, by all means go for it and stick to a program. But if you'd like to roll the dice on a little racing adventure, you've definitely come to the right place.

My philosophy is that the Big Guy or Gal up above gives each one of us only a finite amount of running miles per lifetime. Why waste 'em? That's why I race a ton. Every single time I run, someone gives me a t-shirt and sometimes a medal. How cool is that?

Speaking of t-shirts. A lot of folks don't like to race because they don't think they are fit enough. Wrongo! When you run a race, it doesn't matter how big a pathetic loser you happen to be. The t-shirt the first-place person gets is exactly the same as the one you get. So, say they win the race. You ever see how many folks are still there when the awards are given out? Usually, it's just the guys who happen to be asleep in the park and the families of the guys and gals who won the trophy. And they were forced to get up early to join their significant other. Meanwhile, you've been out of there for an hour and you're already at the pancake house devouring round two of chocolate chip pancakes. Don't forget, you just raced. And for your special day, make sure not to forget the whipped cream!

Two-time Ironman World Champion Scott Tinley and I were racing the Sri Chinmoy Swim-Run event in La Jolla, California. As he was lapping me during the six one-mile run loops on the beach, he goes, "Man, we suck!" I had to laugh. I yelled, "Scott . . . I have ALWAYS sucked. You used to win but now you don't.

Welcome to my world; welcome to Suckville!" Trust me: If you never win, you'll be much happier. Hey, think of trying to get a trophy through security and then stuffing it in the overhead compartment. Now that really sucks!

Don't think of these events as "races." That can totally scare you off. They are just "catered workouts." As you run mindlessly along, someone will hand you something to eat and drink. Does that happen when you go for a run from your house? Hardly.

I look at energy gels a little differently than most people. To me, each gel signifies a workout I probably should have done. I figure if I have a gel every half hour or so it's not only a nice treat, but I've now got another workout under my belt.

When we do the Elvis gig at a Rock 'n' Roll Marathon event, usually we stop and walk and play air guitar with each band every mile or so. That gets the lactic acid out of our legs. Instead of running the same pace and tiring those particular muscles, we are stopping and walking and then starting up again. Usually we can run a 4:30 marathon or so taking all these breaks. Plus, we end up passing a lot of folks during the last six miles who have toasted their legs and are now forced to stagger in. If you haven't trained, walking a minute or so at the end of each mile (starting with the very first mile) is the key.

How do you define success? Here's something to think about: Your buddy is running 50 miles per week to get ready for a marathon, plus riding the bike 50 miles and spending time in the gym. Figure that's 14 hours per week of training or 56 hours per month. You, on the other hand, are running 10 miles per week and doing an indoor cycling class or two, plus maybe a bodysurfing session or two. That's seven hours per week or 28 hours per month. During your buddy's 16 weeks of training, he or she has logged 224 hours while you have put in 112. Your buddy runs a 4:10 marathon; you run a 4:30. Simply put: Your buddy spent 112 extra hours, or over four and a half solid days, to beat you by 20 minutes!

So while you're congratulating your buddy on the whipping you just took, try hard not to laugh out loud.

Then head home and plan out how to avoid training for your next marathon.

WHY IT'S GOOD TO BE BAD

It's important in life to remember that you can always make lemonade no matter how bitter the lemons you happen to be sucking on. Yeah, it would be nice to go to races, go fast, get lots of applause and return home with trophies. But take it from someone who has spent the majority of his endurance sports life bringing up the rear of the pack: The upside of racing on the crappy side of the street is really not that bad. Here's why:

- I'm sure I get a better tan during most marathons or triathlons than most people. It just makes sense. Since I'm out there WAY longer, I become WAY more bronze.

- I hear people after races mumbling about other runners tucking in behind them during the windy parts to get a little relief from the breeze. I know you might find this surprising, but I've never had to deal with that. No one has ever drafted behind me.

- If the marathon costs me $100 to enter and I'm out there an hour or three longer than everyone else, I definitely get more value for my investment.

- Before the race, while the top guys in the age group are busy not making eye contact with each other because they've got their Eye of the Tiger thing going, everyone is happy to chat with me. When you're no threat, everyone loves you.

- If I'm doing a triathlon, I never have to worry about which rack I placed my bike on when I get out of the water. Nope. I just look for the only bike that's still there.

- Also, since I am in the water longer than most, I get to spend some up-close-and-personal time with the lifeguards since they are forced to hang with me before they can breakdown the course. I found out that one of the guys is a waiter at Outback Steakhouse, and after the race I got a coupon for a FREE Bloomin' Onion. SCORE!

- The aid stations are never crowded when I get there.

- The people who get the most applause as they cross the finish line are the really fast athletes and the really, really slow ones. It takes a lot less effort to be the latter.

- I've yet to have anyone ask me for an autograph or training secrets.

- The top guys and gals have to figure out how to haul their brand new trophy home. I don't.

- Finally: By being lousy, you know you can leave as soon as you finish the race. Why wait around to get an award when you can be at In-N-Out Burger downing a double-double?

TAKING IT FROM SPORTS

There are so many great things that come out of participating in running, cycling and triathlon events. But how cool would it be if we could take some of the positives from our sports and move them into real life? Now we're talking!

Aid stations. I don't know about you, but I think it would be awesome to have aid stations all over town on a regular basis. How many times have you been walking to an appointment and feel the urge for a few chocolate chip cookies, a pretzel or two, a cup of Gatorade or, if things are really stressful, maybe a few dinosaur Gummy Bears.

Special needs bag. You're sitting in a meeting and the guy is duller than your father-in-law. You are about to go face first into the table and your eyelids are dropping faster than Martha Stewart's stock. What to do? Hey, what if there was someone to hand you a special needs bag? A Red Bull, a 180, some Jolt Cola, maybe even a concoction we used to use at Ironman we called The Bomb. What was The Bomb? Well, we had it waiting during the Ironman at about mile 20. After 2.4 miles of swimming, 112 miles of cycling and with only 6.2 miles to go in the marathon, sometimes you need a tad bit of a rush. We'd take some defizzed Coca Cola, add some NoDoz and then mix in some aspirin. If your heart didn't explode, that last six miles went by pretty darn fast. The only negative? If the race was on Saturday, you were so wired from The Bomb that you didn't sleep until maybe Wednesday unless you put duct tape over both eyes.

Transition area. In triathlon it's where you go to change from a swimmer to a cyclist to a runner. How cool would it be to be able to go into a transition area to change careers from P.E. teacher to pilot to doctor? By eliminating all the books and tests and studying, you'd save tons of money and oodles of time. Just change clothes and you're in! You could also invite your current flame into the transition area to tell him or her that you're moving on, that you'd like to hang your bike on a different rack, so to speak.

Bodymarking. Ever wonder why the whole world doesn't wear nametags? Here's the solution, except that by taking bodymarking into the real world it's actually better. On the back of your calf you could not only put your age but also some really beneficial stuff: I'm 25 years old, independently wealthy, I love Twinkies – I don't care that they are flush with weird chemicals and have the shelf life of forever, I have no Unabomber-like family members and no weird diseases.

Medals and t-shirts. This has been totally overlooked. When you run a 10K, you get a t-shirt. Close a big real estate deal? You get bupkis, nada – nothing except cash. T-shirts for everything you do plus medals for everything you do well.

Massages. After every race they have folks there to give you a well-deserved massage. After every proposal your neck has to feel tighter than one of Sammy Sosa's corked bats. Massages for everyone!

Brain. This is a great concept from the Urban Challenge. The event consists of two people, 12 checkpoints, trivia, cell phones and a unique combination of running and using public transportation.

After taking a trivia quiz to seed you and your partner, the two of you set off to find 12 checkpoints around the city by figuring out clues along the way and taking digital photos of you and your partner at the checkpoints. It's hip, it's cool, it's a blast. If you need help during the race, you can call anyone you like from a cell phone. Your "Brain" is sitting at a computer ready to answer anything and everything. Say you're at a party and you're trying to impress someone who is into French art. To you, French art is a Jerry Lewis film festival. The solution? Call your Brain to have all the blanks filled in for you.

Skipman. This is another new entry into the endurance sports vocabulary from the Urban Challenge. Besides the Brain, Kevin McCarthy, the creator of Urban Challenge, has added another really cool element to his event. Before the race, you are introduced to a person called the Skipman. His or her picture is actually on your passport. If you spot the Skipman anywhere on the course and take his or her photo, you get to skip the checkpoint of your choosing. Imagine spotting the Skipman on the way to see your accountant and being able to blow off your taxes that year? Or spotting the Skipman at an Ironman and being able to blow off the last 10K of the marathon? Or when you were in high school and ended up playing Nintendo all night and sort of forgot to prepare for that oral report on the history of the snail darter? Find the Skipman and sleep in, dude!

BABBITTVILLE

Since I have been involved in the wonderful world of endurance sports for the better part of the past three decades, I have decided that it was about time to secede from the Union and create a paradise of my very own. Of course, if you would like to come and inhabit what I shall call Babbittville with me, I would love to have the company.

So what would this place be like? I am so glad you asked!

If you are participating in an event, no one else from your age group would be competing so that you would always come home with the biggest medal. Even better? The other people from your age group could come, but they would simply be there to stand on the sidelines and cheer for YOU!

All marathons would be flat and short.

All cycling roads would have large shoulders and be slightly downhill. The drivers would all be polite, there would be no debris or potholes and the wind would always be at your back.

Wherever you go during your hot training rides or runs, someone would be there with a big smile on their face to hand you a cold sponge.

The weather would always be so nice in Babbittville that there would never be a need for gloves, bike shoe coverings, hats or arm or leg warmers.

The ocean would always be 72 degrees and crystal clear; and anytime you were in the water, the sun would always be out.

Any event you enter would provide a cooler-than-cool medal no matter how you do.

Port-a-potties would always be right there, no one would ever be in line and they would be spotless.

Broken bike seats, flat tires and broken spokes would be unconstitutional.

Sunblock would never drip into your eyes.

Every event would have a post-race massage table and would always be open and ready for you.

My apologies to our buddies in sports medicine, but no one gets injured in Babbittville – ever.

The only Performance Enhancing Drugs allowed would be Pop Tarts, Slurpies and anything with the word Hostess on them.

The only big gray things in the ocean would be dolphins.

Women would finally realize that guys having soft abs and muffin tops are actually really good looking.

Your legs always feel fresh and springy.

The words *bonk* and *cramp* would cease to exist.

In a triathlon, the transition area would be 10 steps from where you park your car and 10 steps from the beach.

Instead of cut up bananas, oranges and bagels, the post-race spread would always feature tri-tip sandwiches, Tater Tots and cold beer.

Everyone in Babbittville would always wear a name tag.

Finally, everyone is friendly to each other in Babbittville. If you say "hi" to a fellow cyclist, he or she will always smile, wave and say "hi" back . . . even the roadies.

CHAPTER 4

Bob Babbitt and Shasta

ALL IN FUN

RAT TALES

THANK YOU . . .
THANK YOU VERY MUCH

THANK YOU . . .
THANK YOU VERY MUCH – PART 2

MAKE MY DAY

"MAH" HORSE

AN E-TICKET RIDE

LONDON CALLING

KNUCKLEHEAD MOMENTS

MR. ED EXTRAVAGANZA

THE DIRTY DOZEN

MY BUCKET LIST . . . NOT!

CHAPTER 4 – ALL IN FUN

"When you make the decision to pull on that magical white jumpsuit and wig, grab your inflatable guitar and actually run as Elvis, you are automatically the world's biggest star."

– Bob Babbitt

RAT TALES

Let's see . . . do I have everything? Shorts, running shoes, camera, book, bike, spare tubes, helmet . . . rat . . .

Rat? You betcha! Juvenile? Probably. One of the necessities of travel in the 21st century? Definitely. Forget the laptop, the PDA and the iPod. One of the best inventions known to man is the quivering, God-that-thing's-disgusting $29.95 rat.

It's funny. In our business, we deal with hundreds of daily e-mails, magazine deadlines, print quality, distribution, websites, event planning, race expos, lots of meetings, profit margins and so much more. All that stuff we can't ignore as adults too often gets in the way of the motto we lived by as kids: Who the hell can I nail and how often can I do it?

My rat, Willard V, travels everywhere with me. He's always in my bag and is very low maintenance. Willard takes two AA batteries and a flick of the switch, period. He's very big for a rat, and he lies on his side like he's sick or hurt. The red blood accent around his mouth is a nice touch, but Willard only looks real when he starts to quiver. Hence the AA batteries. Hence people running around like chickens with their heads cut off when they spot him.

That's when the fun begins.

Willard has traveled the world. At a trade show in downtown Chicago, a group gathered around Willard II and tried to figure out exactly what disease he had. After a triathlon in Borneo, the locals figured he fell out of a tree. Ditto in Tahiti and Brazil and Costa Rica.

Like a lot of people we know, Willard is most effective in dim light with a sprinkling of dirt on his back.

At my sister's house (relatives are always an easy mark), she had animal control on the phone, plastic gloves on her hands and a shovel in tow when I picked Willard up by his tail and she ran screaming into the house.

Before the Ironman parade in Kona, a group of 20 surrounded Mr. Rat and tried to figure out exactly what type of rat he was and where they should bury him.

You're probably wondering what happened to Willard I. In a gross case of mistaken identity, Willard was lost at sea in March of 1993. It was 5 a.m., and 500 of us were on the boat heading to the start of the Catalina Marathon. Willard was minding his own business, lying at the foot of the stairs to the top deck, hoping to catch some rays. A few shrieks and startled leaps from passersby satisfied all of us early morning yuksters.

Then one guy decided he was John Wayne. He stopped and eyed Willard cautiously. He stooped and stared for what seemed like forever. Then, fast as a cobra, he struck. Boom! He snatched Willard by the tail and flung him off the back of the boat. I remember glancing out to sea and spotting Willard momentarily on the surface, rolling with the swells, before he disappeared from view. John Wayne, smiling like he had just saved the world from imminent doom, headed upstairs – chest out, chin high. Our hero had flung my $29.95 rat to a watery death.

Hey, I understand the rules of prankdom. Confucius say, "He who lives by the rat occasionally dies like a rat."

But for every time someone actually cuts Willard's head off with a shovel or flings him overboard (which is how we got to Willard V), there are many more times that Willard or one of his heirs creates enough of a rhubarb to justify his continued existence.

Like the evening in downtown La Jolla. A group of us were riding cruisers through town a few days before Halloween. It was about 9 p.m. and I removed Willard from my pack, flicked on the switch, dropped him onto the sidewalk in front of a flower stand, pulled over and waited for the games to begin.

A group gathered immediately. The skateboarders arrived first and surmised that Willard had been struck by a car. Then the flower stand owner came out to see about calling the rat removal squad. Bandana in place over his mouth, he picked Willard up using a broom and a dustpan when I casually mentioned that the rat was indeed rubber and not a real menace to society. The man put Willard down, examined him more closely, laughed and returned to his stand. The skateboarders wanted to know where to buy a Willard of their very own.

As the group dispersed, I went to retrieve my pet. A woman who had been on the outskirts of the group stepped right in front of me and let me know what she really thought about Willard and his act.

"That's sick!" she shouted at me. "That's really sick!"

I smiled.

Hey, isn't that the whole idea?

THANK YOU . . . THANK YOU VERY MUCH

Let's be honest. Sometimes it just feels good to be a little goofy no matter how old we happen to be. If you're in college, a college dropout, a college "student" on the 10-year-to-life ultimate dorm-party plan or a college professor, to relieve the stress that sometimes sneaks up on all of us is definitely a good thing to do. Running, of course, is an awesome stress reliever. Running a race dressed up as Elvis? Besides zapping stress back to the dark ages, it will be the absolute best day of your life. When you make the decision to pull on that magical white jumpsuit and wig, grab your inflatable guitar and actually run as Elvis:

- You are automatically the world's biggest star. No rehearsals and no playing small time clubs. Nope. Everyone from age 5 to 95 knows The King by sight and will be cheering your every move.

- You will understand what real celebrities go through dealing with the paparazzi. Every time you turn around someone will be pointing a camera in your direction. How cool is that? Other runners will actually run backward in front of you in hopes of capturing your really hip image on their point-and-shoot cameras for posterity.

- Time becomes irrelevant. In fact, who wants to finish fast when you can have more fun running your slowest race ever?

- You can run as either a thin or chubby Elvis. If you are skinny, you can be the young Elvis. If you are in the muffin-top Hall of Fame, you're the middle-aged Elvis. No matter what your size, sex or heritage, you too can be King for a Day.

- The miles will fly by so fast you won't believe it. Between "thank you, thank you very much," and a few verses of *Jail House Rock* and *Return to Sender*, by the end of the race your voice will be more worn out than your legs.

- You will bond for life with the folks dressed up as Batman, Superman, Spiderman, Idiot Guy and all of the other Running Superheroes.

- You will actually start to look forward to wearing white Lycra in public and won't quite understand why anyone would wear just a running top and shorts any longer. How dull can one person get?

- You are totally incognito and unrecognizable – all dressed head-to-toe in white Lycra. You might as well be in witness protection. If you sing lousy and dance even worse? Bring out your inner Elvis and go for it!

- You'll know you're really hooked when your need-to-bring list on race morning includes not only BODYGLIDE®, shorts, heart rate monitor and running shoes but also a sequined cape, pompadour and really large gold-rimmed sunglasses.

THANK YOU . . . THANK YOU VERY MUCH – PART 2

"You are a beach ball with lips!"

I am dressed in what was a few minutes ago a very nice white Lycra one-piece jumpsuit accented from head to toe with gold striping down the sides. But after just a few miles, my Elvis 'do, chest, legs and gold-framed shades and, yes, my prized white Lycra jumper are coated in an off-brown off-the-charts form of sludge, dirt and slop known affectionately as Marine Corp Recruit Depot merlot.

A nice bouquet? Whoaaaaahhh. I think not.

"Pick it up, fat boy. You were faster when you were dead!"

Okay, I should have known. I signed up for an event called the Boot Camp Challenge with a few thousand other what-the-heck-was-I thinking everyday folks. It consisted of 3.1 miles of running and wall climbing and crawling and pushuping and situping.

Did I mention that the Marine base also invited lots of guys in starched brim hats that make their living staying up late and getting up early so they can make your day just a little bit more miserable? They are called Drill Instructors – D.I.s if you've never been in the military; something a lot worse if you have. For the politically correct crowd, they are probably referred to as Doctors of Intimidation, and their prescription for everything in life is always the same: When in doubt, yell really loud and kick the living crap out of everyone and anyone. Sound like your mother in law? Go with that thought. Then multiply by 65.

"Hey, Elvis . . . did somebody super-size you when you weren't watching?"

They were the kids in second grade that stole your lunch and sold it back to your parents. Then did it again the next day. They would hit you so hard when you played battle bombardment that the name VOIT would still be tattooed into your forehead for your first date and your high school graduation. They pantsed you so often, your picture in the yearbook was of you in your underwear, and you were voted the kid most likely to be arrested on a morals charge.

"The King???? Man, if you're The King, I'm the frickin' Pope!"

Dressed as Elvis, I don't "blend" well. When I'm running a Rock 'N' Roll Marathon, people cheer and laugh. Here at MCRD? I am easy pickins', the Woody Allen look alike and the second grader with glasses, high-water pants, shoes with animals on them and dollar bills sticking out of my pocket, and the Please Abuse the Crap Out of Me post-it note on my back.

I am the prize catch in the herd, and every doctor in the house wants to be in on the operation.

"Big E . . . That's no push-up . . . that's a WUSSUP!!

I think I have set a record. I have now climbed the same wall 12 times and have splinters in places I didn't think small pieces of lumber could ever penetrate. I have hit the deck for 20 push-ups so often, three weeks later my arms are still set in the same vibrate mode as my Barcalounger.

"Priscilla is on the line. She wants to know if you'd like her to come do your push-ups for you."

The answer is yes. Get Priscilla to drag her lazy butt down here and join me for a fun day of abuse.

But if she wants to stay home from next year's Boot Camp Challenge, no worries, I'll give out her phone number. I'm sure these doctors would be happy to make house calls.

MAKE MY DAY

I've been staring at the same weeds and dirt now for what seems like hours. I take that back. Since my face is barely millimeters away from said weeds, the correct terminology is probably "living in" rather than "staring at."

I twist my head slightly and glance at my mud-encrusted Timex to see how long I've actually been motionless. Hmmmm. A full 2 minutes and 30 seconds of lying facedown in this clump of weeds, my heart racing at something approaching the speed of sound and my breath hurtling out of control like a runaway Hoover.

In college I prayed for a high draft number so I wouldn't have to fly off to some distant rice paddy to crawl on my belly like an iguana and be scared to death 24 hours a day. Today I spent $35 for the opportunity to do just that.

My latest move was to crawl up some stupid hill, keeping all my moving parts as close to the ground as humanly possible while three maniacs with red armbands tried to shoot me full of holes. My purpose? Why to stay alive and capture the flag, of course.

The name of the game is paintball. It was April 1992 and I went as a guest of TYR, the swim-product manufacturer, which has an annual paintball shootout with their friends. The professionals from Fields of Honor provide both teams with paintball guns, eye protection, ammunition, CO_2 cartridges and full instruction. Plus a fair amount of fear. "Remember, NEVER take off your goggles," says one. "A paintball will definitely pop your eye right out of its socket. Okay, let's play!"

Great. A group of guys and gals in full military fatigues equipped with weapons that can desocket an eyeball. What if one of these people had a really lousy day yesterday and needed to vent some frustration?

I've never had an overpowering urge to be a walking paint canvas for colored bullets that cover 200 feet per second. Co-star in *Boyz in the Wood*? Not me. My philosophy is the same as paintball specialist and then Los Angeles Raiders owner Al Davis: "Just run, baby."

The teams split up, the red team heading to their fort, the yellow team – the good guys – convening at ours. David Rosen of TYR divided us into small groups and made battle plans. One group would head up to the hills and work its way through the red team's defense to the flag. Another would dig in to repel the enemy advance and guard our flag.

Rosen's group (with me in it) would head up the valley into the heart of enemy fire and just bull our way forward.

Important things to remember? Number one, that eyeball-leaving-the-socket deal. Number two, the paintball has to explode on your body and leave a paint mark the size of a nickel for you to be eliminated. If it just hit solid and left a welt the size of Vermont, you were just maimed. Words like "wasted," "snuffed," "whacked" or even "killed" are considered inappropriate. "Eliminated" is the proper term.

If you cock and shoot too fast, a paintball could explode in the gun. "To keep your gun functioning correctly, remember to occasionally swab your barrel," one of the Field of Honor instructors reminds us. Who is he kidding? Isn't that what Pee Wee Herman was doing in that theatre in Florida?

Each clip of paintballs contains seven or eight bullets. The CO_2 cartridge is good for maybe two clips before it fizzles out. Having to remember when to reload makes the game exceedingly stressful.

Imagine running through the forest, eyes darting quickly right and left, and paintballs zipping by your head so close you can feel them. Suddenly confronted with an enemy, you panic. When was the last time you changed the CO_2? Do you have any bullets left? Are your goggles on? How high is your pain threshold? Do you really care that much about capturing some old flag?

Obviously my answer was yes to the last question.

I crawl and scramble behind enemy lines to the top of the ridge where I lie flat, pondering the botanical wonders of the weeds embedded in my left nostril.

Bullets whiz past, and I wonder how much flatter I can get. I wonder where the heck my arms and legs are and what's in the line of fire?

"I know he's all alone up there," yells one of the red-banded assassins down below. "Let's all charge him at once and shoot him in the head!" screams another as they all laugh.

"Go ahead," I think, "make my day."

I make my move, bolt upright and scramble to higher ground. Just like Clint Eastwood and Rambo. I am untouchable. Uneliminatable.

I turn and set up in a shooting position as one of my attackers runs toward me. I draw a bead and fire. My gun makes a small pop, and I know I'm in deep doo doo. A paintball rolls to the end of the unswabbed barrel, hesitates momentarily and falls uselessly into the high grass.

My eyes meet those of my assailant through eye-socket-protecting goggles. He smiles. I don't.

I'm eliminated in a hail of paint, one bullet exploding on my upper left thigh leaving a bruise I can still see three days later. The last time I saw marks like this was when I played racquetball with my Uncle Phil and hit the ultimate kill shop, whacking him smack dab between his lower cheeks. The ball stuck and Uncle Phil was left with a matching set of hard-to-explain bruises. It was the shot of a lifetime.

Because I've been marked, I have to depart the Field of Honor with my weapon held high over my head to identify me as eliminated. I trudge over to the out-of-bounds area where all the eliminatees gather to share war stories.

We can hear shouts out on the field. "Gotcha!" "You missed me!" "It didn't break, man!" "Hey, that's only a splatter mark!" And "You're dead, dude!"

Five minutes later, we're all alive and reloaded. It's a brand-new game – and a chance to get even.

I change my CO_2, reload, tug my goggles tight and head back into the hills to re-examine the greenery.

Make my day, you red-armbanded punks! Nobody – and I mean nobody – paintballs Clint Rambo Babbitt twice in one day!

"MAH" HORSE

It was about 10 a.m. on a Saturday. I was out on a bike ride through Fairbanks Ranch just north of San Diego. Thirsty, I stopped at a small deli, bought myself a soft drink and sat on the curb in front of the store to relax a bit and soak in a little early morning cloud cover. My bike was left leaning against a post.

Suddenly, a large Ford pickup truck, circa early 1970s, pulled up and slammed to a halt. Out stepped two cowboys. The driver was about six-feet tall and looked like the Marlboro Man. His buddy extricated himself from the cab and ambled slowly out of the passenger door, doing a great Gary Cooper High Noon imitation. Tiptoeing on his spurs, he stood all of five-foot-three. His blue jeans were somehow able to traverse the twisty and turny legs of a guy who I'm sure was voted most likely to be a walking croquet wicket by his high school class.

He came sauntering over. Weight to the left leg . . . weight to the right leg . . . weight to the left leg . . . weight to the right leg . . . He stopped momentarily in front of my bike, eyed it up and down and then headed inside.

The two soon emerged with two cases of beer. While the driver packed the beer in ice in the bed of the truck, Mr. Bow-Legged stopped to closer examine my steed. His hat (he had a small head... maybe only an eight-gallon hat) was pulled down to cover one eye. A toothpick dangled from a Continental-divided-type gap between his two front teeth, and a belt buckle the size of Vermont with a picture of a bucking bronco on it divided his thickly muscled upper body from those I-can't-believe-those-babies-can-keep-him-upright legs.

"How much does this thing weigh?" he asked, pushing his hat up.

"About 22 pounds," I answered.

He circled the bike, pointing to the handlebars. "What the heck are those for?"

"Well, they're supposed to put you in an aerodynamic position," I answered. "I guess they make you go faster."

"When Ahh want to go faster," he said, "Ahh just give mah horse a little love tap with mah foot." He tilted his head back and laughed, his toothpick now angled skyward. "That usually gets her movin.'"

"Ahh don't understand why anyone would want to ride a make-believe horse," he continued as he pointed derisively at my bike. "You could be riding a real one."

The challenge was set. He was daring me to step across the line.

"Well," I said, "do you carry a spare shoe with you in case your horse comes up lame? If I get a flat tire, I have an extra tube."

The toothpick was now moving at 100 rpm.

"Ya can't carry a whole helluva lot with you on that thing, now can ya?"

My serve: "I bet my monthly bill for chain oil is a little less than yours is for hay and feed."

His serve: "You prob'ly go through a lot of those skinny little tahres (tires?)"

My serve: "Yeah, and I bet it's lots of fun to clean up after a 1,200-pound horse all day long. Do you buy your pooper scoopers at Shovels R Us?"

His serve: (A big smile.) "You can't go nowhere 'cept concrete with those skinny tahres, now can ya?"

Now I had him. Game, set . . . match?

"Have you ever seen a mountain bike?" I asked. "They have knobby tires and three chain rings. You can climb up anything on one of those guys."

He paused and circled, circled and paused. He pawed at the ground with his right boot. The belt buckle was now directly in the path of the cloud-shrouded sun, damn near blinding me.

"Ya know," he said, "Last winter Ahh was riding in the snow near mah house. I remember thinkin' how great it was to be out there where no one else could go. Ahh came over this rise and, sure enough, there was one of those mountain-type bikes."

I smiled. He was all mine. When it comes to debate, he'll know to never, ever mess with this cowboy again.

"The bike was on its side," he said. "It was 35 degrees out, snowin' and the guy was standin' there shiverin' tryin' to figure out how to make that darn thing move."

A long pause, toothpick down to 75 rpm. Another big smile.

"That's when Ahh know why Ahh don't want to be ridin' no make-believe horse. If you break down in the middle of the woods on your bahcycle . . . you'll starve to death.

"Me? I'd just eat mah horse!"

AN E-TICKET RIDE

We arrive in the mountains east of San Diego and unload our beasts. It is our usual threesome: Larry White, king of the flats and the downhills; 70-year-old Jack Wilson, king of the mountains; and yours truly, the king of lunch and hanging on for dear life.

In the back of my mobile toy box (aka my Mitsubishi), we have three road bikes, lots of running and cycling shoes, fins, goggles, a wetsuit or two, a very dusty battery-controlled rat for scaring anyone and everyone, and my 12-wheeled downhill grass sled (not my best use of $80). Along the floor are assorted spilled bits and pieces of energy gels, bars, stuck-together salt tabs and, of course, Pop Tarts, the world's most perfect food.

Yes, I know, Pop Tarts are the Velveeta of pastries with the same nutritional value and the shelf life of forever. But during a long ride when you can put a Brown Sugar Cinnamon Pop Tart in the back pocket of your jersey and wait for it to heat up to exactly the right temperature, there is no bigger treat on the planet. One question, though: If we can invent the digital camera, e-mail and Guitar Hero, why can't we figure out a way to build a toaster mechanism into the back pocket of our jersey so we can place said Pop Tart back there and simply wait for it to pop up, toasty, crispy and . . . perfect?

Once during a ride, a buddy and I discussed for a full three-mile climb the things we would like to change about the world's most perfect food. Why can't they frost both sides of the Pop Tart? Why not frost the little pastry outcropping that surrounds the meat of the Pop Tart?

But I digress . . .

The plan is to ride 50 or so miles starting at 4,000 feet, head west to Highway 79 and then take Sunrise Highway up the 11-mile climb that takes you over the top of Mt. Laguna at 6,000 feet before the free-fall back through the spectacular pine trees to where it all began.

I pull my bike out of the car and my tire is as flat as defizzed cola. Since I own just one set of wheels and they happen to be for sew-up tires, I pull the spare tire out of its cobweb-encrusted bag and start to unroll it. This doesn't look good. I'm thinking this sew-up dates back to the first Bush administration. I do my best strong-man imitation and try to stretch the old warhorse onto the rim. Since it's already 90-plus degrees and I'm coated with sunscreen, the sweat is pouring down into my eyes making it tough to get a grip. Finally, the tire is on and secure.

But suddenly, we all stop in our tracks. There it is, just like when you're 17 years old and set to go to the prom. A zit. But not just any zit. The king of all zits. Zitzilla always shows up on the tip of your nose, at the end of your chin or smack dab in the middle of your forehead right before the big dance. Forget Clearasil. This thing is bigger than Guatemala. There is not enough of the pink stuff to cover this big of a surface. The comb-down to cover the forehead zit works for a while, but eventually it will unveil itself at the worst possible time.

I am 17 once again. But Zitzilla is not on my face. It's sticking out of the side of my tire. Remember, this is my spare so there is no net here. If I flat during this ride, there is no one who can help me; no bike shops here. And who the heck else is carrying a spare 26-inch sew-up? Yep, I'm hosed.

"I've ridden lots worse-looking tires than that," Jack growls.

"Are you sure?" says Larry. "It looks pretty bad."

"Get on your bikes and let's go," insists Jack. "It's not getting any cooler out here."

So I mount up. On the flats when Larry takes off, I stay with Jack. When the road points skyward, I stick with Larry. But here's my dilemma: If they both get away and I flat, the next thing you know a coyote or mountain lion would be flossing with my bones. Not good.

I decide that to be on the safe side, I need to stay in front of them both so that if I do flat they will see me. Then they'll be obligated to at least hang with me for a little bit before laughing and pointing and disappearing over the horizon.

I'm getting the sense that my zit is reaching its popping point as we turn south and start up Mt. Laguna. The heat is intense, my heart rate is pegged, the vultures are circling and the tire pressure is building. Suddenly, my zit explodes and the boys hear it from 400 yards behind me.

"Man, that sounded like a shotgun blast," laughs Jack. "I'm amazed that tire lasted so long. I bet you got 20 miles out of it!"

Great. I'm only 30 miles from the car. Now what?

We discuss it for a while. They'll take my car keys and ride ahead. I'll try to flag down a car. They'll get back to the car and come looking for me. Sweet! Only one problem: I haven't seen a car in 40 minutes.

I'm walking uphill in my socks, the thermometer is heading north of triple digits, and I'm hoping to find some stranger to give me a ride to safety.

After about 20 minutes of hoofing, a mirage approaches from behind. It's a California Highway Patrol cruiser. I wave him down and he stops. He tells me that as much as he'd like to help me out, their policy is to never pick up people. He will call it in and send for help though. He starts to pull away and then stops and backs up.

"Hop in," he says. "I'll take you to your car."

We load my bike in the trunk and start to chat. Turns out that the officer is a long-time cyclist and has done the Rosarito to Ensenada Bike Ride a number of times. This is nice. The cruiser is air conditioned and this beats the heck out of walking with my bike on black pavement in socks.

Then the call comes in. A car T-boned a motorcyclist back on Highway 79, and he has to respond. But he's in a quandary. He can't just dump me on the side of the road, can he? Nope. He agrees to take me to the Laguna Mountain Store before responding, but he has to step on it. The sirens and flashers are going full-bore as we hit 90 and fly by Jack and Larry. They never see me. The officer pulls onto the gravel at the store going about 50 miles per hour, leaving a huge dust cloud that envelopes everyone sunning on the front porch. I jump out and grab my bike and shoes as he U-turns and disappears.

"How is everyone?" I say with a big smile as I walk up to the store. "Man, that was some experience!"

Silence. Mouths open, but too scared to talk. Families huddle together for safety. The people on the porch just witnessed a police cruiser with lights and sirens dump off a guy they now think is public enemy number one (me).

"Yeah, I had this flat tire and the officer was kind enough to give me a ride and then he got an emergency call . . ." I start to explain. I can tell from the looks on their faces that whatever I'm selling, they aren't buying. I walk into the store and get the same cold-shoulder treatment.

Just then a truck pulls up. It's a couple with two small kids. I wander over and explain my situation. They're heading down the hill and are kind enough to offer me a ride. Of course, they weren't witness to the commotion and the fact that everyone else thinks I'm on a wanted poster. Nope. They're just stopping for a treat before heading home after a weekend of camping.

I walk into the store with my new family and guess where they're headed? Yep, straight to the Brown Sugar Cinnamon Pop Tarts.

We load my bike into their huge truck. I'm in the passenger seat nibbling on the world's most perfect food, knowing that I have had a day for the memory bank: A flat tire led to Zitzilla, which then led to an E-ticket ride with the CHP and then an air-conditioned ride back down the mountain to my SUV.

My new family drops me off and we exchange phone numbers. They're from Orlando and end up coming to our Muddy Buddy event at Disney World the next year. We're now buddies for life.

When Jack and Larry arrive back to the car, they find me stretched out on a wide slab of rock catching some rays with a big smile on my face while my Pop Tart sits next to me as it assumes the perfect temperature.

It's funny. The great thing about cycling is that sometimes not knowing where your ride will take you makes the experience that much tastier.

LONDON CALLING

To Whom It May Concern:

I am looking at a map of the world. Man, there are a ton of little countries out there – nothing personal if one of these slightly-bigger-than-Shaquille O'Neal countries is yours. I was thinking that there must be some nation – maybe yours – that's in need of a slightly used triathlete for the upcoming Olympics in London.

Okay, so I'm more than slightly used. I've been doing this sport since 1978, and I freely admit that I rode a bike with solid rubber tires and a radio bungee-corded to the handlebars at the 1980 Ironman. But, as they say in the used-car business, I may have been dented a few times over the years, but I've never been hit solid.

As soon as I heard the 2012 Olympics were going to be in London, I started wondering: How long does it take to become a citizen of Mozambique? And does anyone in Somalia do triathlon?

I want to march in the opening ceremony, maybe even carry your country's flag. I want to party with the NBA guys and talk transition with Bob Costas. I can show Bob how to strategically apply BODYGLIDE® without being arrested.

NBC could do an up-close-and-personal on me, and I could talk about how motivated I am to represent your country.

I promise to go hard in training and memorize your anthem.

And I vow to use my favorite-ever Olympic line after my disappointing last-place finish.

The medal ceremony will be over and my competitors will be out partying. The transition area will be empty. The world will be tuned in to swimming or gymnastics. I will be seen in the distance staggering toward the finish, sun setting and firmly grasping my cramping hamstring.

The tears will be everywhere as I enter Olympic Stadium. After I elbow the steeplechase guys out of my way to get to the line, I will collapse in a heap on the track. Cameras will zoom in, and I'll have the perfect answer when the assembled media ask why I put up with this torture rather than dropping out: "[Your country's name here] did not send me to the Olympics to *start* the triathlon," I'll sob. "They sent me here to *finish* the triathlon."

Now, if you could just point out which multi-colored 3-D landmass is yours, I can start rehearsing my lines and we can get this show on the road.

Hope to hear from you soon!

Olympianingly yours,

Bob

KNUCKLEHEAD MOMENTS

When we celebrated the 20th year of *Competitor* magazine in 2007, I felt the need to honor not just our greatest athletes but also some of the greatest knuckleheads and knucklehead moments that I have been oh so proud to witness. We'll start with me . . . as I've got WAY too many stories to share. A couple of my personal favorites? Glad you asked! Here are a few:

Second-Place Weirdo
Years ago, I put together a relay team for the Santa Barbara Triathlon. Since the relay teams way back when took off with the pros, for some reason, when our cyclist tagged off to the runner – me – we were in first place. Why I was designated as the runner is anyone's guess. So not only was I running, but folks along the way had to be thinking I was the overall *leader* of the race. SWEET!

Just past seven miles or so while I'm waving to my fans and kissing babies along the way, the real leader (a guy named Scott Tinley) approached from behind. Without breaking stride, Tinley pulled my running shorts down to my ankles right before an aid station. I was no longer the cool guy in first place. I was the second-place weirdo trying to cover up and run at the same time.

Padding It
Of course, this next one I did totally on my own and really have no one to blame. I went to Spin class one morning and maybe I was a tad tired. All I know is that halfway through the class I was out of the saddle climbing my brains out and happened to look down and notice that the pad on my bike shorts was on the OUTSIDE of my shorts. Hmmmm. I don't think that was a very good look.

Paper Trail
Along those same lines, six-time Ironman Champion Mark Allen remembers this one time when he was at a race and felt that for some reason people were staring at him more than usual.

"Well, I'm wearing number one," he said to himself. "I'm sure I'm the favorite to win so everyone knows who I am. That must be why so many folks are staring."

No such luck.

Just then a friend walked up and gave The Grip the real scoop:

"Dude . . . you've got toilet paper stuck to the bottom of your shoe."

Number 25 the Hard Way

Bobby Lopez had done every Catalina Marathon, and this particular morning he would be running it for the 25th year in a row. What an awesome accomplishment! One problem: It's a point-to-point course, so you have to take a 5 a.m. boat to the start of the race. It was now 6 a.m., and he was still in his hotel room bed in Avalon. So what does he do? He laces up his shoes and runs the course in reverse from Avalon to Twin Harbors to keep his streak alive.

"When I started seeing other runners on the course, they all kept yelling 'You're going the wrong way!' Hey, I thought to myself. Tell me something I don't know!"

Maybe Get It to Go Next Time?

Speaking of Catalina . . . Jeff "The Rat" Atkinson, a finalist at the 1500 meters from the 1988 Olympics, was leading the marathon during his first attempt. He and his buddies would traditionally go to Catalina for the weekend but always ran the 10K then headed off to a local watering hole called The Sand Bar at about mile 25 to make fun of the marathoners as they staggered by.

Since he was now one of those crazies actually running 26.2, he wasn't about to break tradition. Even though he was LEADING, The Rat stopped at mile 25 to have a beer with his buddies. Now well-hydrated, The Rat cruised the last mile to win by about 30 seconds.

Groundhog and Shadow

We have an event called Ironman Revisited that race director extraordinaire Rick Kozlowski ("Koz") and I created a number of years ago. The idea was to go back to Oahu, the site of the original Ironman, and have folks bring their own support crews and complete the original Ironman course without aid stations, blocked off roads, splits, cheering crowds or cutoff times.

Since Koz and I had both participated in the 1980 Ironman on Oahu, we thought it would be a cool fundraiser for the charity that we created with Jeffrey Essakow, the Challenged Athletes Foundation. We wanted folks who to come to Waikiki and relive a little bit of history.

One of our original participants in Ironman Revisited was Sid Jensen and went by the code name Groundhog. He brought his brother, Greg Jensen (code name Shadow) to be his support person. Groundhog did the entire event in his board shorts while Shadow followed behind. The two carried personal walkie-talkies to "communicate" along the way. Groundhog came out of the water after the 2.4-mile swim and headed out on the bike. Shadow headed over to Denny's for breakfast. Groundhog was 40 miles into the bike ride, out of water and stuck on the side of the road with a flat.

Shadow was still in Denny's.

Eventually Shadow finished up his breakfast, found his stranded and slightly frustrated brother, and Groundhog got back on the road.

A little later during the bike ride, Groundhog needed a little nourishment.

"Gu, Gu, Gu!" he yelled into his walkie-talkie.

Shadow thought his brother was saying "Go, go go!" and took off, leaving Groundhog supportless once again.

Eventually everything worked out fine. Groundhog finished Ironman Revisited before midnight and even gave Shadow his finisher's medal in thanks for being his crew. The next day. I asked Shadow what he thought of the job he did.

"Well," he said, "if being a good crew is a jockstrap . . . I guess I was a thong."

Hey, Happy Pants!

Earlier I mentioned two-time Ironman champion Scott Tinley and how he pantsed me at the Santa Barbara Triathlon. Did I also mention the time he bungee-corded me into a port-a-potty before a race? I think 10 years of therapy has helped me deal with that one.

Well, as they say, revenge can be oh so sweet. One day, I was driving along the coast and was stopped at a light. Who should I see but Scott Tinley out on his bike. He comes over to the driver's side, and we chat for a while. He then pulled out in front of me, balanced on his bike, pulled down his shorts and mooned the world.

While this was going on, he didn't happen to notice the police car that had pulled up to my left. All of a sudden you could hear over the loud speaker,

"Hey Happy Pants . . . want a ticket?"

This time it was Tinley's turn to cover up.

MR. ED EXTRAVAGANZA

His name was Shasta. He had four legs, a huge head and John Elway-sized teeth. Little did either of us know at the time of our first meeting that he would have a huge impact on my life.

The time frame was the mid 1980s and the location was a series of trails out in the Cleveland National Forest east of San Diego. I was what you might call a running guy back then who had completed the

Ironman Triathlon a few times but really spent more time running than riding or swimming. At that point in my life I was a physical education teacher at a small private school, so I spent my days playing capture-the-flag, dodgeball, elbow tag and street hockey with kids from age 4 to 12. I would play games from 9 a.m. to 2:30 p.m. every day and then go off with my buddies and run, ride and swim until it got dark.

As you might have guessed, life was pretty sweet!

Then a friend called me one day and asked if I would like to be on a team for an event called Ride & Tie. Each team consisted of two runners and one horse and the concept was fairly simple: One person starts off on the horse and rides a few miles, ties the horse to a tree and starts running.

The partner starts off running, finds Mr. Ed, mounts up and starts riding until he passes his teammate, then ties up the horse again and takes off running.

You would repeat this scenario for 28 off-road miles. It sounded like a lot of fun.

One issue: I had never actually ridden a horse before.

So the week before the event, my partner – who was more of a horse guy and less of a runner – and I met up to take his horse Shasta for a little pre-race get-acquainted spin.

I wore a helmet and mounted up. When I wanted to turn left, I pulled the reigns that way. Ditto for turning right. It was like taking my driver's license test without the severe arm pit sweat, the cracked rear view mirror or, most importantly, a brake pedal.

I was actually feeling pretty confident as we geared up for the start on race day. Hey, how tough could this be?

Then I heard an explosion. Instead of a whistle or a hand signal or maybe someone whispering the word "GO," the Ride and Tie was started with a shotgun blast. By the time I reached the horse formerly known as Shasta at about mile five, he was pawing at the sky with his front hooves and smoke was coming out of both nostrils. The transformation from Shasta to Lightening was complete, and for the life of me I couldn't figure out how to get this 2,000-pound creature calmed down enough to allow me to mount up and get my butt in the saddle.

When I did get on, Lightening became Carl Lewis and jumped anything and everything along the path. I was holding on to his mane with both hands for dear life and, when my eyes weren't totally closed, I could see that the entire landscape was a blur as we flew by the other runners and riders at something close to the speed of sound.

All I could do was pray that he would eventually tire and that I could somehow parachute off, tie him up and get safely back to running.

By mile 15 we were in a groove. I was riding as little as possible, my partner was riding as much as possible and Lightening had, now that he was a little fatigued, become the mellow Shasta.

After running about 15 of the first 20 miles, I was actually starting to look forward to the final 8 miles of this Mr. Ed Extravaganza when I could finally stop running and simply cruise in on Shasta's back and take in the scenery.

Not so fast, Cowboy Bob.

As I approached the check point at mile 20, I spotted Shasta being loaded into the back of one of those little horsey trailers. Hmmm. This is strange. Did someone not let Shasta know that this was a 28-mile race, not simply a 20-miler?

I spotted one of the handlers and asked politely what was going on:

"What's happening with Shasta?" I screamed. "Where the heck are you taking him?"

"We're taking him back to the start," said the horse whisperer. "His hooves are sore."

Shasta was looking right at me now, and I could see a little smile forming at the corners of his really huge lips as he was eased into the trailer.

"Are you KIDDING me?" I stammered. "MY feet are sore. Get him back out here so I can ride this last eight miles!"

As you might imagine, they could have cared less. A little laughter and a lot of pointing was all I came away with. Yep, they were pointing in the direction where I needed to head to finish up the last part of the event. By myself. Without a horse. And yes, on really sore hooves . . . I mean feet.

As I ran that last section of trail, I thought about the day and the event. Man, I really enjoyed the concept of two runners taking turns running and riding. But the idea of including a 2,000-pound beast with a mind of its own to me was a tad flawed. What if I adapted this concept, dumped Mr. Ed, Shasta and Lightening, used a mountain bike instead, added some obstacles, mixed in a mud pit and a beer garden – plus costumes and off-the-hook team names – and give it a go?

So in 1999, we did our first-ever Muddy Buddy event with 250 teams and 500 participants in San Diego, California – six miles, four obstacles, one awesome mud pit and thousands of amazing memories for everyone involved. Now we have Muddy Buddy events all over the country with thousands of fun-loving mudaholics joining us in the coolest mud pit on the planet. (I'm easy to spot because, since this is a leapfrog event, I'm the idiot in the bright green frog outfit greeting all the folks as they slither through the mud pit.)

Come join us. Bring your best buddy, your running shoes, your mountain bike and your let's-have-a-good-time-attitude.

But do me a big favor: Leave the horse at home.

Editor's Note: *For more information on Muddy Buddy, go to www.muddybuddy.com. Be sure to register early, since every event sells out.*

THE DIRTY DOZEN

Okay, so you've been putting a race number on every weekend since Bill Clinton was inaugurated. You've run so many 5Ks and 10Ks that you know every inch, of every race course on your local circuit. The St. Patrick's Day event kicks off your season every March, and before you know it the summer is over and you're sitting with six t-shirts and you can't remember anything from those race days besides that early morning alarm, the start, the finish and spending two hours afterward trying to remember where the heck you parked.

Yes, it is true. You can run long and fast and hard pretty much every single weekend – which is exactly why the Grand Muftis of running created 5Ks and 10Ks in the first place.

But what if, rather than staying on life's straight and narrow sidewalk, you wanted to veer far off the pavement and do something totally silly? Sort of like forgetting the steak and potatoes and kicking off dinner with a hot fudge sundae. That's right. Do the unexpected, be crazy, seize the moment and smile all day long.

Sound good? It is.

The Muddy Buddy Ride and Run Series was created for all of the reasons listed above and more. Why should you grab a buddy and give a Muddy Buddy a try? So glad you asked! Here are 12 dirty reasons:

#1 - History. The founder of Muddy Buddy – me – once did an event called a Ride & Tie with two runners taking turns running and riding a horse. After riding a 2,000-pound thang anxious to throw me to the ground and dance the four-legged cha-cha on my head, I decided the concept was awesome but would be a tad better if Mr. Ed stayed at home. That, of course, led to the first-ever Columbia Muddy Buddy.

#2 - The buddy. How fun is it to do an event with your husband or wife or your kids? Especially since most of the time we are totally selfish and participate in endurance events by ourselves. Not with Muddy Buddy. It's two runners, one mountain bike, and you take turns running and riding and leapfrogging your way through about six miles. You bond with your teammate and savor doing something together for a change.

#3 - Anyone can do it. Six miles? Come on. Each teammate runs about three miles (one mile at a time) and rides three miles (one mile at a time). ANYONE can do that! The fast teams go about 40 minutes, the average teams take 65 minutes or so, and even the slowest teams finish in 90 minutes. You know the old philosophy, right? No long hours and no light stick means no problem!

#4 - Costumes. Yep, you and your buddy can dress up and be totally incognito. Elvis works, as does the Incredibles and Thing One and Thing Two. The costume contest at Muddy Buddy is almost as entertaining as the race itself.

#5 - Decorate. Since you'll be sharing one mountain bike, there is a good chance that it belongs to one of the buddies. Which means the other buddy is seeing Mr. Bike for the very first time race morning. To avoid the "I ran right by the bike" scenario, you can decorate your bike right on site. Besides now being awesome looking, it's cool to keep the tassels and colored duct tape on your bike even after race day because it's so distinctive.

#6 - Beast. If you and your buddy together weigh in at 400-plus pounds, you qualify for a very special division called the Beast Division. One caveat: Don't think you can simply TELL people you guys weigh over 400 combined. If you place top three, you will have to get on the scale during the awards and prove your heft. Weigh 398 combined? Prepare to be booed off the stage. One team in Boulder a few summers back was so worried about making the 400 barrier they each ate a full Marie Calendar pie right before the race just to be on the safe side. The positive? They definitely weighed north of 400. The negative? They finished sixth and out of the medals.

#7 - Family. Besides you and your wife or husband or dad or brother or sister competing together (the minimum age is 14), there is also a Mini Muddy Buddy for kids ages 4-13. Hey, moms and dads, here's a good-to-know tip: There are definitely showers after the race. If you are going back into the mud with Junior, save the first shower and live in your mud-coated body until the Mini Kicks off. Who the heck wants to take TWO showers in the same day?

#8 - Mud. At the end of the day, that's what it's all about. College professors, brain surgeons and bill collectors share one trait: They all like to slither through a really slimy mud pit and be a kid again. At the start of the race, you'll be 35 years old. By the time you get to the mud pit? Maybe 8. Which might explain the flying mud balls and the WWF action that seems to always occur in the mud pit.

#9 - Obstacles. Every mile or so there is something fun, like a 25-foot inflatable with a cargo net up the front and slide down the back. That is the place where the cyclist will drop the bike, conquer the obstacle and start running, and where the runner will conquer the same obstacle, grab the bike and ride past his or her partner before the next obstacle. There are a total of four obstacles before the teams reach the brand new 20-foot wall climb and the mud pit. The key? When you are the runner, after you come off an obstacle, don't forget that you are now the cyclist and need to take the bike with you. Forgetting Mr. Bike can be a HUGE mistake.

#10 - Medals. Everyone gets a finisher's medal at Muddy Buddy. The idea is to smile and enjoy and finish. If that happens and you go three for three? You get a medal.

#11 - Training. Why bother? An indoor cycling class and a run or two and you are golden. If in doubt, see number 3.

#12 - Charity. The Challenged Athletes Foundation (CAF), www.challengedathletes.org, raises money to keep disabled athletes in the game of life through sport. The Columbia Muddy Buddy contributes greatly to that fund-raising effort.

MY BUCKET LIST . . . NOT!

Many of us have put together an awesome list of must-do running events and categories that we would eventually like to do before heading off to that ultimate finish line in the sky.

In putting together mine, I got to thinking . . . What attracts me to do an event and what doesn't? Since the attraction part is easy, I figured I'd share some of my thoughts on the types of events that I have absolutely no interest in doing.

Unknown Distance
I'm not a big fan. If the event is one of those multi-day deals where you have absolutely no idea how long you'll actually be out there, I'm out. I really like the concept of 70.3, 6.2, 26.2 or 13.1 so I'll know approximately how long I'll be suffering. As they say in racing, pain is temporary. I'm just one of those people who really wants to know just how temporary.

Self-Contained
I like the idea of someone handing me a cup of water, gummy bears, pretzels or a peanut butter and guava sandwich every once in a while. If there are no aid stations and I need a Sherpa, I'm out.

Lost, Sleep Deprived and Hungry
This again may explain why adventure racing went the way of Bernie Madoff's stock portfolio. Besides way too much gear and way too many logistics, a lot of us simply don't get the concept of paying an entry fee to be cold, wet, lost, hungry and sleep-deprived for an undermined period of time. Who ever thought that would catch on?

Cold Water
The first out-of-the-area triathlon I did was in Hawaii. My type of races showcase sun, warm oceans, lakes or rivers and post-race drinks with umbrellas by the pool. Cold water is for drinking, not for swimming in. Think ice cream headaches, numb feet and fingers and major shrinkage. 'Nuff said'.

Death Valley
I know. The idea is to challenge yourself. But when the location of the event is Death Valley, Slit your Wrist Falls or Fall off a Cliff Summit, I head in another direction.

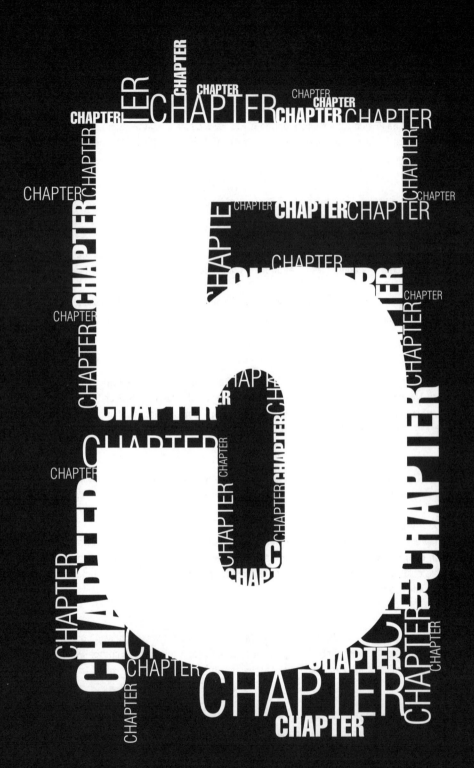

Bill Walton and Scout Bassett

PERSEVERANCE

HE SHOCKED THE WORLD

LUCKY 13

FEAR THE KNIGHT

"I GET TO RIDE MY BIKE TODAY"

MILE MARKER 86

CATALINA MAN

NO LIMITS

CHAPTER 5 – PERSEVERANCE

"Having my leg amputated gave me hope. It opened up the door for me."

– Karen Aydelott

HE SHOCKED THE WORLD

You can practically feel Marc Herremans' joy in his finish-line photo. It's one that does indeed tell a story. He is ecstatic, triumphant. It was a breakthrough race on the world's biggest stage. For the Belgian, the 2001 Ironman World Championship was the ultimate coming out party.

His bib number was 1114. Seeded? Not quite. Heck, the guy's bike was barely in the parking lot. But he finished sixth. Nope, not sixth in his age group. Sixth against the biggest names in the triathlon world. He went 8:51:19 on one of the toughest days ever.

Herremans was now someone to watch, someone to look out for and someone to fear.

Then came a fall off his bike while training for Ironman Lanzarote on January 28, 2002. He was now unable to walk, paralyzed from the waist down. The doctors told him that he'd never walk again. That he'd never swim or be athletic again. That he should stop taking his vitamins and antioxidants and take their medicine instead. That, because he was now in a wheelchair, his friends and girlfriend would soon desert him.

The doctors were wrong. His friends never left his side, and he and his girlfriend later built a house together. He threw their medicine away and kept taking his vitamins.

One year after his biggest triumph – and a mere nine months since his biggest trauma – Marc Herremans returned to Kona on October 19, 2002 to once again tackle the monster known as Ironman.

Unfortunately, he had stomach problems and dropped out after the 2.4-mile swim. But just getting to the starting line and through a tough swim was a victory in itself. He returned that afternoon to the Ironman finish line to great everyone who came across.

It was bittersweet. He loved the high of the finishers, but he hated not being among them. Marc Herremans vowed that he would be back – and that he would finish.

In Belgium he is a bigger hero with bigger impact than ever before, and Christopher Reeves – an American actor and director who became a quadriplegic after being thrown from a horse in May 1995 – became his friend and supporter. (Reeves later died on October 10, 2004.)

In training Herremans reshaped his body. Every week he rode 300 miles on his handcycle, swam 9 miles and pushed his wheelchair 60 miles.

The Ironman is unique, special. The hellacious winds combined with the heat of the lava fields can rub you raw and snuff out your will. But in the end, the Ironman is strictly personal. It is not you against your fellow racer, it is you against the course . . . you against you.

On October 18, 2003, Marc Herremans swam 1:02:35 for 2.4 miles, finished the 112-mile handcycle in 8:11:56 and went 3:33:23 in his racing chair for 26.2 miles. His total time was an amazing 13:24:25.

As an Ironman rookie, he shocked the pros. In 2003, he shocked the world.

Editor's Note: *Marc Herremans returned to Kona again in 2004, 2005 and 2006. In 2006, he became the first wheelchair athlete to arrive at the finish line, crowning him Ironman Champion. In 2003, Herremans started a foundation called "To Walk Again" that supports other disabled people with efforts such as creating a sports center for disabled people and investing in bone marrow research. For more information, go to www.towalkagain.be/.*

LUCKY 13

The year was 1997. The voice of Ironman, Mike Reilly, and I were taking turns bringing the best age-group athletes up on stage at the Ironman World Championship. That brief moment in the spotlight serves as reward for the mind-numbing training days that everyone who places there has endured.

What has always impressed me is how normal, everyday folks balance their training around family, work and everything life throws at them in order to change the perception of how fast a 40-, 50-, 60-, 70- or 80-year-old can race 140.6 miles in the stifling heat and horrific winds of the Kona coast.

That year, a 51-year-old woman named Karen Aydelott from Pasadena, California (by way of Minnesota) stood on the No. 1 spot when her division was called. She had just gone 11:49. In her career, she has completed 27 Ironman-distance events, and this would be her only win in Kona in 12 attempts.

Her first triathlon was in 1984 in Minneapolis. On race morning, she woke up early so as not to disturb her husband and two sons, took the baby seat off the bike and rode over to Lake Harriet for the women's-only event.

Aydelott won her division and was home to make breakfast and greet her family before anyone knew she was missing. "I was pretty excited," she admits.

Her first race in Kona came in 1989, and in October 2012 she attempted her 13th Ironman World Championship, this time at the age of 66. The last time she raced in Kona was in 2005.

On June 22, 2006, while doing a bike workout around the Rose Bowl in Pasadena, she was run over from behind. She remembers nothing but was told that she was flipped over the top of her bike and then dragged under the car. She emerged with back issues, road rash and an ankle that suffered an explosive break.

Like a typical triathlete, she got right to the point with the doctor. "I'm an athlete," she remembers telling him. "I need to get back to training, so let's get this show on the road."

After looking at the X-rays, the doctor was blunt as well. "Karen, you were an athlete," he said. "I doubt if you ever will be again."

Aydelott endured eight operations before she realized it was time to have the talk. "We had discussed amputation early on," she recalls, "but now I knew that it needed to be done. I wanted to get back into triathlon, and I couldn't do that without the amputation."

Two years after the accident, she had her right leg amputated below the knee. "Having my leg amputated gave me hope," she says. "It opened up the door for me."

There were challenges. She had to clip in and out with her left foot and deal with the fact that it takes 30 percent more energy to power a prosthetic. Aydelott's goal wasn't to get into Kona through the Physically Challenged (PC) Lottery. It was to get there by qualifying as an age-grouper in her division. "I'm conceding nothing, and I knew that I would never give up."

She didn't qualify in 2010 at St. George or Arizona but Aydelott knew that things were looking up when she was able to get out of the saddle and charge. "Okay, I'm back," she said to herself. "I'm me again."

In November 2011, Aydelott qualified for the 2012 Ironman World Championship by winning her division in Arizona with a time of 16:10:32. "Getting back to Kona is a dream come true," the now San Luis Obispo, California, resident said before leaving for Hawaii. "I can't wait for race day."

Editor's Note: *Unfortunately, Karen Aydelott was unable to finish at the 2012 Ironman World Championship and had to drop out after mile 19 of the run (15:34:56 into her day). Incredibly, she went 1:25:14 in the swim and 7:27:05 for the bike.*

FEAR THE KNIGHT

Steve Brenneck lives in a square. There is no kitchen and no bathroom and barely enough room for a bed, a dresser, a closet and a place to hang some shirts and a few pairs of pants. Most of the people who live in this senior hotel in downtown San Diego, California, have been down on their luck for quite some time and have no family or friends to help them out. It is a depressing place to visit and an even more depressing place to call home. These are the people whose hopes and dreams simply did not pan out. They are society's outcasts – each and every one.

I take that back. There is 66-year-old gentleman who calls this place home, but he spends as little time there as humanly possible. Each day that he laces up his running shoes is a day in a time machine of his very own. He was born in Seattle, arrived in the San Francisco area in 1950 and has been on his own since sixth grade. There is a self-imposed fog surrounding what happened in his formative years to drive him from his home, siblings and parents and why he never attended either high school or college. He would rather not talk about it, and I would rather not push.

"I grew up on my own and hitchhiked across the country a number of times," admits Brenneck. "I would work in a department store, stock shelves or unload trucks, but there were a lot of times I had absolutely nothing in my pockets."

Not much has changed. Today [November 2007] he gets $940 a month from Social Security and pays $500 for his room. That leaves $440 to live on each and every month.

In prior days, he could get a bed at the YMCA for $10-$12 a week. A self-taught musician, he would make some spending money in the local bars playing the piano.

"I couldn't read music, and I learned to play by ear," he says. "My preference is show tunes, and I guess you could say my style is like Liberace's."

He certainly didn't ever live like Liberace. He lost his car when he was 54 years old and had to walk to get to his infrequent jobs.

"I would live wherever I could find a place," says Brenneck.

One day, he started running from BART Station to BART Station up in the Bay Area and loved the feeling of speed. At the age of 55, he noticed the athletes from UC Berkeley over at Edwards Stadium and wondered if he could run with them on the track.

"They didn't seem to mind, so I ran intervals with the track team," he continues.

When he moved to San Diego in 1999, he jumped full on into the running scene and had immediate success. There were training sessions with Kevin McCarey and Paul Greer, two coaches who helped him out because they knew that Brenneck had talent but little else. At the age of 61, he ran a 5K in 18:58 and was second in his age group at the Carlsbad 5000. His personal best for the 10K is 39:48.

It's ironic. Brenneck lives in a place where most everyone is heading downhill fast.

"It's one of those places where everyone is dying," he says. "I know it's coming, but I don't want to face it right now." He smiles. "I feel like I'm still kicking ass."

He definitely is.

Greer and Peter Gregory, the coaches of the San Diego City College cross-country team, needed to build a team of good runners, so they decided to tap into a card-carrying AARP member who could keep up with the youngsters. Brenneck started taking music classes at the college and learning theory.

His teammate Tom Kee talks about the energy that Brenneck brings to the team. "He's always the first one out at practice and the last one to leave," says Kee.

Rico Eckard, a former high school 4:02 miler who is also a little long in the tooth to be back in junior college – he ran at San Diego City College back in 1990 and 1991 before heading off to Desert Storm and 10 years in the service – feels that Brenneck brings a special character to the team.

"I watch his form," says Eckard. "It's flawless."

When Brenneck put his race uniform on for the first time, he had a hard time controlling his emotions. He had to wait 66 years to get his first uniform.

"I almost went off into the woods and shed a few tears," he says softly. "The athletes and coaches have been so supportive. Living and eating at a senior center is depressing. There are so many seniors who are not motivated to do anything, who feel they have no reason to live."

Brenneck started out dead last, but passed 11 runners in his first junior college cross-country meet.

"I have plenty to live for," he says. "I feel like I've found the Fountain of Youth."

His teammates call Brenneck their little brother and the ladies man.

"When we go out," says Eckard, "two or three women are always hanging around Steve."

They are putting in 60-70 miles per week with plenty of hills and tempo runs. There are 14 members on the team, and they try to do their long run of 13 miles together every weekend. They train, they race and they bond. But eventually they go their separate ways, and Brenneck trudges back to the reality that he lives in every day.

No one in the senior center knows about his other life. They have no idea that Steve Brenneck's secret to staying young – to try to turn back the hands of time – is to become a member of the San Diego City College Knights cross-country team.

When he is at home, the night is the time when he is alone in that bare room and tries his best to ignore the sadness and depression that envelopes him on all sides.

During the day, he is a hard-charging Knight.

Scratch that. An ass-kicking, hard-charging Knight.

"I GET TO RIDE MY BIKE TODAY"

Bill Walton is a basketball legend. He led UCLA to 88 straight wins and two national titles. He was the number one draft pick of the Portland Trailblazers, led them to the NBA championship back in 1977 and was the most valuable player of the championship series that same year. He won another NBA title, this time with the Boston Celtics, in 1986. At 6-feet, 11-inches, he is undoubtedly one of the greatest basketball players in history. He was named to the NBA's 50th Anniversary All-Time Team despite the fact that, in a career marred by injuries, he played a total of only 488 games while missing 680.

As fans and amateur athletes, we tend to put professional athletes up on a pedestal and wonder how cool it would be to live that life.

Be careful what you wish for.

Walton has two fused ankles and has suffered through 36 surgeries in his 58 years. He had to give up his career as a basketball analyst because his back issues were so severe he not only couldn't get on a plane, he couldn't leave the house. For two years he basically was forced to live on the floor of his San Diego home, crawling to the bathroom and eating his meals there. The pain in his back was excruciating. "I wasn't living," he admits. "Every day was worse than the day before."

It got so bad that he actually contemplated suicide.

But then the miracle: Surgery number 36 helped to eliminate the nerve pain that was so debilitating and would just never go away. Walton was finally able to get off the floor and live his life again. Gradually he started working out, taking trips to the gym to swim and lift light weights. Then it was time to dust off his bike, his favorite of all workouts, and get back on the road.

To this day, Walton's feet are still so bad that he can't use cages or clip-in pedals. He uses flat pedals that allow him to push down but not pull up. But he could care less. He just wants to be on his bike.

As you can imagine, at nearly 7-feet tall, his bike is huge.

But the best part of it now? His smile is just as huge.

He joined the Challenged Athletes Foundation for their San Francisco to San Diego Million Dollar Challenge Bike Ride, October 16-22, 2010. Seven days and 620 miles later, Bill Walton was as happy as he's ever been. "I have my life back," he says. "I'm the luckiest guy in the world."

During the ride that raised over $1.35 million dollars to help disabled athletes get the sports equipment they need to stay in the game of life, the weather was horrific. The rain came down in buckets and there was so much debris on the road that the group of 140 riders had north of 200 flat tires during their trip south. But not one of those riders who raised at least $10,000 each to be a part of the week ever complained. How could they? There were amputee athletes and paralyzed athletes riding the same roads under the same conditions as able-bodied athletes, and if they could suck it up and handle being soaked to the bone, so could everyone else.

Plus, there was a really tall guy who would come down to breakfast every single morning with a twinkle in his eye and that megawatt smile that lights up every room he enters and, no matter how horrific the conditions outside were, he'd simply lift his arms up over his head and say over and over and over again:

"I get to ride my bike today."

What could be better than that?

MILE MARKER 86

It was the day after the 2008 Ford Ironman World Championship. David Bailey, who had been one of the best motocross athletes on the planet before he was paralyzed, was barreling down the Queen Kaahumanu Highway on the Big Island of Hawaii heading back toward beautiful downtown Kailua Kona. He had never expected to be on his handcycle again, to be pushing hard again and to experience the joy of sweat dripping from the brim of his helmet into his eyes again. "God, this feels good," he said to himself. "One day I have to come back and do this race again."

Just past the Kona Village Resort he spotted mile marker 86 and everything in his life that has happened to him since 1986 suddenly came flashing back. A smile played at the corner of his lips. He had honeymooned with his wife, Gina, in October of that year at the Kona Village Resort and had watched the Ironman live for the very first time while Dave Scott won his fifth Ironman title. He told Gina that one day, when his motocross career was behind him, he needed to come back and try the Ironman.

He was coming off the best motocross season of his life and doing the Ironman seemed like it was a long, long way away.

But in a sport where catching big air is the name of the game, suffering through a big landing is something everyone hopes to avoid. In January of 1987, Bailey was paralyzed from the waist down while training for the Supercross season opener. At the time, he was the defending national champion, making a high six-figure salary with a new wife, a new house and plans to race in Europe later that year. The world was his oyster. The next minute, Bailey's career was over and he was another disabled guy trying to figure out what his new purpose in life was.

"When I was injured, I had already accomplished a lot," he says. "Everything I wanted to win I did, so I definitely went out on top. But when you are a professional athlete, you're pampered and everyone is doing things for you. When I was hurt, I was pampered even more."

He ignored what they told him in rehab. "I thought I'd be back walking soon, so why bother?" he admits. "What made me great at motocross didn't transfer to dealing with a spinal cord injury. I needed to focus on what I *could* do, and eventually I realized that if I didn't get it together I would lose everything."

He was a husband and a father and a motocross star without a career. And he was upset and depressed and didn't have a clue how to deal with it.

Then he met Jim Knaub, a former Olympic Trials pole-vaulter who had been paralyzed in a motorcycle accident as well but had realized pretty quickly how to adapt to his new surroundings. "Jim told me he didn't care who I was or what I'd won," he recalls. "He gave me the tough love I needed."

Just a few days after they met, Bailey joined Knaub for a road trip to Mexico to go deep-sea fishing and ride four-wheelers. Knaub, a five-time Boston Marathon champion in his racing chair, pushed Bailey to get into that sport as well. The next thing he knew, the two of them were off to Australia to do an event, give skydiving a try and then race the Boston Marathon. Knaub brought out the athlete that had been lying dormant inside of David Bailey.

Then it happened. Wheelers were trying to finish the Ironman under the cutoff times using a handcycle for the 112-mile bike portion and a racing chair for the 26.2-mile marathon. A goal of Bailey's that dated back to 1986 was back in play. He went over to Hawaii in 1997 to watch John Maclean from Australia try to become the very first wheeler to finish the Ironman officially. In his previous two attempts, Maclean had missed the bike cutoff time of 5:30 p.m. On this day, though, Maclean made all of the cutoff times, and Bailey knew that when he came back in 1998, it would be his turn.

During his three year run in Kona, Bailey took third, second and, in 2000, first. His nemesis all three years was Navy SEAL Carlos Moleda, who had been paralyzed when he was shot in the back during a military operation in Panama. Bailey had beaten Moleda at the Buffalo Springs qualifier in Lubbock, Texas, in 1998 and thought the Ironman was in the bag. Not quite.

"I got smoked," he recalls. "I was on the Queen K Highway during the handcycle. I'm in the lead, and one of the able-bodied guys in the race comes by and goes, 'Hey, you guys are doing great.'"

"I'm thinking, 'You guys? . . . What do you mean you guys. It's just me out here.' I asked him what he meant and he goes, 'Oh, he's a ways back.' So I relaxed. Five minutes later Carlos comes by me like he's on a scooter. I'm wondering what 'a ways back' meant to that guy on the bike?"

Carlos Moleda ended up getting the better of Bailey in both 1998 and 1999. But after coming from behind and finally beating Moleda in 2000, Bailey felt like that chapter in his life was over. He beat the course record holder – the guy he went to bed every night and woke up every morning thinking about; his whole family was there; and race day turned out to be his mom's birthday.

What could be better? Mission accomplished.

A few years later, Bailey met a 16-year-old motocross star-to-be named Ricky James. The kid had a great name, great looks, a megawatt smile, a need for speed, and he was fearless. "He just had it all," says Bailey.

Then, like Bailey, James was paralyzed. It happened during one of his first races after signing a pro contract. But James, unlike Bailey, dove back into life right away. A month after the accident he was in Las Vegas riding the roller coaster at New York, New York and cruising around a motocross event on a four-wheeler. A year after his accident, James was back on a motorcycle on the same track where he was paralyzed. He was the Go for It Kid, and the fact that he got back on the motorcycle proved to Bailey that he could get back on the bike and ride a few laps himself.

Not good. When Bailey got back on the motorcycle and rode around the track, he aggravated a pressure sore. What would have been a small issue became a big one, due to the fact that he was older, wasn't eating well, was sitting a ton and traveling a lot. When the pressure sore became infected, financial and insurance issues kept Bailey from getting the help he needed. His weight dropped from 155 to 120 pounds and he laid facedown in a pillow for the better part of a year. "I was heading south fast," he says. "I was dealing with wound-care clinics, insurance issues and my legs were frozen at the knee joints so I couldn't bend them at all. Everyone was concerned, and with good reason. I was hanging on by a thread."

It was two years before he could sit up. And without the help of the motocross community, he would have lost his home. "What I learned from the suffering I previously put up with while training and racing Ironman got me through those tough times," says Bailey.

It didn't hurt that when he finally was able to have successful flap surgery and the infection cleared up, Ricky James, who he mentored in motocross, showed an interest in triathlon.

The next thing he knew, Bailey was pushing his handcycle again alongside James and feeling like a new man. "Training with Ricky was everything in terms of my recovery," he says.

And training with Bailey, who had records of every workout he did to get ready for Ironman, got James to the finish line in Kona, October of 2008, in 12 hours and 44 minutes – his very first attempt in his third-ever triathlon. "Whatever David told me to do, I did," says James.

While James was off adding to his growing tattoo collection the day after that 2008 Ironman, Bailey (who didn't race this year) was back where he belonged, hammering away on the Queen K Highway – not because he needed to prove anything to anyone, but because getting ready for the Ford Ironman World Championship made him feel vibrant and oh so alive.

"When I got back home from the trip," he recalls, "I told Gina that I think I'd like to come back and try the Ironman again."

Bailey went back to Lubbock, Texas, on June 28, 2009, and nailed down his Kona spot at the Buffalo Springs Lake Ironman 70.3 and taking second pace.

"I am so excited to be doing the Ironman again," says Bailey.

And why shouldn't he be?

Life is great, the guy is healthy and mile marker 86 is out there waiting for him.

Editor's Note: *David Bailey returned to Kona in October 2009 and raced in the Handcycle Division of the Ironman World Championship after a nine-year hiatus. He took second in a time of 11:35:38. Pretty amazing, since his time was 11:05:20 when he won in 2000.*

CATALINA MAN

He is lying in a sleeping bag on the side of a grassy hillside. The full moon enhances the stars that surround Bobby Lopez and his fellow Catalina Marathoners. This was in the early days, mind you, when the runners were dropped off by boat the day before the race. This was before the athletes stepped up to hotels and beds and a before-dawn boat trip from sleepy Avalon to the start at the Isthmus.

Back then you camped out near the area called Twin Harbors, got up in the morning and dragged your sore ass across 26.2 miles of off-road hell, gathered your sleeping bag and back pack at the finish and staggered off to the boat for your trip back to Long Beach.

This was three years into the Catalina Marathon's 27-year history. Lopez had eaten dinner and enjoyed a few drinks with the other Catalina Marathon pioneers. There might have been 100 in total. He had ignored the suggestion that they not bring food with them back to their sleeping bags because wild boars, who ran alongside their friends the buffalo, tend to be attracted to anything somewhat edible.

"I snuck these chocolate chip cookies back with me after dinner and had them in my sleeping bag," Lopez recalls. "In the middle of the night, I hear this snorting and this huge thing is pushing me and my sleeping bag down the hill. I opened my eyes and was petrified. It's a huge boar, and he wanted my cookies!"

The 68-year-old Lopez looks much younger than his years and his zest for life is apparent. On March 18, 2005, he ran the Catalina Marathon for the 27th consecutive time. Lopez is a member of a very exclusive club.

His background was karate. During training he was used to running two or three miles. One day his neighbors asked him if he'd run in their school's five-mile fun run. He agreed, but was worried. "To me five miles was like running to San Diego from my home in Los Angeles," he says. "I told my wife I didn't think I could do it. I was so nervous I was up all night."

When he got to the fun run, he didn't have much, well, fun. "Everyone was passing me," he says. "Women, men, heavy guys, bald guys. I fell down once and threw up all over the place. I was trying to stay with anyone who passed me, but I couldn't." He was so embarrassed he didn't stay for the post-run party. "I said that's it, I'm never doing that again. I went home, got some lighter fluid, poured it on my shoes, set them on fire and put them in the trash."

You figured that might be the end of Bobby Lopez's running career, right? Not quite.

He was talked into running the San Diego Marathon. After training for eight weeks for the race, a friend asked him if he had run his 18-20 miler yet. You see, you can't run a marathon unless you've run 18-20 miles beforehand, he was told.

The race was Saturday. So on Wednesday of that week Lopez went off and ran 18 miles. "I'm dying and can hardly walk afterwards," he laughs. On Saturday, in the rain, despite a pre-race meal of nachos and cheesy fries, he ran a 4:05 marathon.

In 1978 another friend told Lopez about a new marathon on the island of Catalina. Since he had never been there before, Lopez thought it sounded like a great idea. He figured there would be cabins over on Catalina, so all he brought was a sleeping bag. But there were no cabins, just a very steep hillside to throw his bag on.

Year two it rained and their sleeping bags started to slide down the hill. The solution? How about some rocks under the bag? Good to prevent sliding, not so great for getting much shut eye. Year three was Lopez's up-close-and-personal visit from the chocolate chip cookie-eating wild boar.

Lopez become an icon of the Catalina Marathon. Every March he returned to the island to run the marathon to keep his streak alive. But then came 1999, the 21st running of the event. By this time, Lopez was staying in town in a warm bed and then taking the boat to the Isthmus, just like most everyone else. But some of the old timers still camped on the hillsides. "When I stopped camping, they started calling me Condo Man," he laughs. As was his habit, Lopez was out partying until about 12:45 a.m. before race day. Hey, at least he wasn't still setting anything on fire.

But somehow he slept through his alarm and woke up at 5:45 a.m. The boat left town at 5 a.m. without him. "Have you ever had your car stolen?" he asked. "That's what it felt like. I'm standing there at 5:45 a.m. looking for the boat, knowing it was gone but not believing it was gone," recalls Lopez. "I'm thinking I've got to do something." He called the helicopter company, but the office didn't open until 9 a.m. Too late. And a taxi couldn't get him to the other side of the island in time.

"So I went to the finish line and got someone to verify my start," he says. "I was going to run from the finish back to the Isthmus. At 7 a.m., BAM! I took off. It was so lonely running up those big hills that you usually come down at the end of the marathon. 'This isn't fair,' I said to myself. 'I'm working my butt off.' It was really boring with no one to talk to."

Eventually he started to see the marathoners on their trek to Avalon. "They're going 'Lopez, you're going the wrong way!' I'm like . . . duh!"

Finally he ran into some aid stations and was able to get something to eat and drink. But then, as he came closer to the start, there were no more runners and the aid stations were all packed up and put away. He found some morsels on the ground and a few half empty cups to drink out of. When he was done, another issue became pretty important to him: Now that he was 26.2 miles away from Avalon, how the heck was he going to get back to town?

"I was lucky," he says. "The sheriff who started the marathon was in his car reading his paper and had fallen asleep. I tapped on the window and woke him up. I told him my story and had him validate my finishing time. I told him that I didn't have any money, and I didn't have any way to get back to town. He goes 'I haven't been to town in a couple of weeks so I'll drive you, but I always stop at the airport for breakfast when I go to town.' So he paid for my breakfast and took me to the finish line where I gave the race director my time and kept my streak alive."

Bobby Lopez loves the Catalina Marathon and this year [2005], his 27th in a row, he took second in his division with a 4:36.

He is asked about the attraction for a marathon that started with a handful of entrants but now sells out with 700. "It's the camaraderie," he insists. "From the beginning, the race drew college professors, car mechanics and electrical engineers. It really didn't matter what you did for a living. All we cared about in those early days was running. People would break out a bottle of Meyer's Rum, and we'd all have a shot right there at the start."

"The only bummer of a streak like this," he says with a smile, "is that you have to come back and do it every year.

"But if I ever miss a year? You can take this to the bank. I am never coming back!"

Editor's Note: *Bobby Lopez went on to do five more Catalina Marathons and in 2010 ended his streak with a grand total of 32 consecutive runs on Catalina island.*

NO LIMITS

The only limits we have are the ones we set for ourselves. – Amy Palmiero-Winters

Amy Palmiero-Winters of Hicksville, New York is struggling through the snow pack early on at the Western States 100 on June 26, 2010. The event features EKG-like peaks and valleys both in terrain and temperature from the start in Squaw Valley to the finish in Auburn, California. Part of the struggle is the altitude in the Sierra, part of it is with traction in the snow and part of it is the fact that her training didn't include much in the way of uphills, downhills or trails for an event that majors in all three because her focus was the 24 Hour World Championship on the roads in Brice, France, six weeks earlier where she ran nearly 124 miles in 24 hours.

Big mistake.

But Palmiero-Winters is as tough as they get. She weighed two pounds, six ounces at birth and was sent home because she kept trying to kick her way out of the incubator. She ran through the brutal winters of Meadville, Pennsylvania; and then, at the age of 22 in 1994, she severely injured her lower left leg in a motorcycle accident. She had 25 operations over the next three years to try and save her leg but eventually had it amputated below the knee.

"Accidents happen," she says, "and, as unfortunate as that was, we all learn from them. The foot was crushed, it was at least four sizes smaller than my good foot, and the ankle had become fused. That caused a lot of issues with my hip and back, and I knew it would be better for me to get rid of the leg. When something like this happens, everyone has two choices: You can give up or you can move on. I'm where I am today because I chose to move on."

Right now she's moving on very slowly, making her way inch by inch up the snow-coated trails. Western States has it all starting with 18,000 feet of elevation gain and 22,000 feet of elevation loss in 100 miles. The start at Squaw Valley is at 6,200 feet, and during the first four miles the runners climb 2,550 feet to 8,750-foot Emigrant Pass. Temperatures range from 20 in the early morning and during the nights to 110 during the heat of the day. Over half of the race for the majority of the runners is done in complete darkness with only the narrow beam of light from a headlamp to guide them. Finish under 24 hours and get a silver belt buckle. Finish under 30 hours and get a bronze belt buckle. Finish one second over 30 hours and you get nothing.

From the age of 8, Palmiero-Winters had been a runner. So while she struggled from surgery to surgery during those three dark years, she focused her goals on getting back to her sport. "My goal after the amputation was to run another marathon," she says.

She went on to become the best female amputee marathoner in the world with a 3:04:16 in Chicago in 2006. When she switched from marathons to ultramarathons, she finished first in the female division at the Heartland 100 Mile in October 2009 and also finished first overall at the Arizona Road Racers Run to the Future 24-hour race on New Year's Eve 2009 where she qualified for the U.S. World Championship team when she ran 130 miles in 24 hours. How good was that? She finished 14 miles ahead of the first able-bodied man and 37 miles ahead of the world-recorder holder able-bodied woman. That's called making a statement.

Palmiero-Winters, who turned 38 on August 18, 2010, is the mother of 7-year-old Carson and 5-year-old Madilynn. They never cease to amaze her.

"One day Carson was riding down the street on his new bicycle, and he pulled up beside a group of kids," she recalls. "He gets off his bike, puts it down, walks up to them and goes, 'Hey, that's my mom. She's the fastest mom and she's got a prosthetic leg.' He was as proud as he could be."

For good reason. His mom was honored with the 2009 Sullivan Award as the Amateur Athlete of the Year and the 2010 ESPN ESPY Award as the best female disabled athlete in the world. Since the beginning of 2009 she has run five 50-mile races, five 100-mile races, three 24-hour races, one Ironman triathlon, three marathons pacing other athletes and four marathons pushing children in wheelchairs. She is one of those people who never lets obstacles stay in the way for very long.

"A friend of mine always asks me, 'Why do you set your goals so high?' And I say 'Why not?'"

Which brings us back to trying to do the unthinkable: No one with a prosthetic leg – man or woman – had ever finished Western States. Pat Griskus, who, in 1985, became the first leg amputee to finish the

Ironman World Championship, had dropped out of Western States. When Palmiero-Winters heard from Robin Griskus that her husband, who was hit and killed by a car while on his bike in 1987, dreamed of one day finishing Western States, the new goal was in place: Finish this one for Pat.

"The event wasn't even in my mind until I met Robin and heard Pat's story," recalls Palmiero-Winters. "That's when I knew I had to do it."

The rules state that you can have a pacer for the last 40 miles of Western States. The race organizers offered her the opportunity to have a pacer right from the start. Palmiero-Winters appreciated the gesture but said no thank you.

"I came here *because* it's tough," she says. "I didn't want any special advantages. I wanted to finish Western States just like everyone else."

The descents were so steep that, because of the pounding on her stump, she spent more time walking down them than running them.

"Everyone was flying past me on the downhills," she says. A long pause. "Then I'd get them all back on the uphills."

At mile 60, she was joined by her pacer, top ultrarunner Heather Perry. They met for the first time on the trail that day and bonded. When they ran onto the track at Auburn High School, the crowd went crazy and Palmiero-Winters, as depleted as she has ever been in her life, started to feel the scope of her accomplishment.

"It was the toughest thing I have ever done, even harder than childbirth," she insists. "It's also now on the top of my life accomplishments, right behind having my children."

Perry was pretty moved herself. It was her birthday, and she said afterward that running around the track with Palmiero-Winters toward that finish line was the best birthday present ever.

Not long after returning home from the race, Palmiero-Winters went to see Robin Griskus and Robin and Pat's daughter, Laura, to present them with the belt buckle she received for going under 30 hours, for going 27:43:10.

"To have that belt buckle in my hands and then to give it away was really hard," she admits.

"But that's okay," she continues. "This year was for Pat, next year will be for me, and I'll try to go even faster."

Editor's Note: *Amy Palmiero-Winters went on to become the first female amputee to finish the Badwater Ultramarathon in 2011 with a finishing time of 41:26:42. For an update on Palmiero-Winters, visit her website at www.seeamyrun.com.*

CHAPTER

6

Rudy Garcia-Tolson

INSPIRING

HOPE

CHANGING A NATION FOREVER

ONE-ARM WILLIE

FLAMINGO TIME

40 DIAPERS A DAY

MR. CLUTCH

LIVING THE DREAM

CHAPTER 6 – INSPIRING

"Sport makes me whole. When I'm racing, I'm the same as everyone else out there."

– "One-Arm Willie" Stewart

HOPE

It is November of 2009. More than 2,000 triathletes are about to jump into the chilly water of Tempe Town Lake for the start of Ford Ironman Arizona. The air temperature is see-your-breath cold, it's still dark, and you don't have to go very far to see the look of terror in the eyes of brand-new Ironman hopefuls.

The announcement has been made that it's time to toss the stocking caps and sweatshirts aside and take the plunge.

One athlete at the back of the wetsuit-clad group stands out from the rest by being shorter than them all. Without his legs on, he's barely four-feet tall. He has long arms and an upper torso chiseled from swimming countless miles. He's one of the most decorated Paralympians around, winning two golds in the 200 individual medley: one in Athens and one in Beijing.

Six weeks earlier he had tried to become the first double above-knee amputee to finish at the Ironman World Championship but missed the bike cutoff time by 15 minutes. It can be tough riding a regulation bike without quadriceps and hamstrings in the heat and wind of Hawaii. But nothing in 21-year-old Rudy Garcia-Tolson's life has ever been easy. A birth defect left him with nonfunctioning legs. He had 15 operations before age 5 that did nothing to help straighten his legs or allow him to be like the other kids. His options? Either live his life in a wheelchair or have both legs amputated above the knee.

He chose the latter. Yep. At the age of 5 he made the choice and his parents and doctors followed his lead. He learned to swim and, along the way, formed a relationship with prosthetist Michael Davidson from Loma Linda University Medical Center in Southern California.

When Sandy, the young man's mother, asked when Rudy would start running after the amputation, Davidson thought she was joking. No double above-knee amputee had ever run, and very few were getting around without a walker.

Davidson remembers his first meeting with 6-year-old Rudy Garcia- Tolson. "I walked in and Rudy was doing a handstand on the walker," Davidson recalls. "I realized then that if he wanted to run, I'd better figure it out."

The two have been working together ever since to improve prosthetics. Rudy would break leg after leg until they were perfect.

"One time Rudy was telling me there was a problem with his walking leg and when I turned it over, Tootsie Rolls fell out," says Davidson, laughing. "I forgot that my collaborator was only 9 years old and was looking for a place to stash candy, just like any other kid."

At this moment in Arizona, Rudy is without legs and walking on plastic stubbies to the water's edge. He makes his way through the crowd and the rumbling begins.

"It's Rudy!" someone yells.

Chants of "Rudy" reverberate and the applause grows louder.

For the first-timers, this day in the desert will be a serious leap of faith. They are scared – and with good reason. In a few minutes they will dive into cold, murky water and attempt to finish 140.6 miles before midnight.

The tension that was so thick just moments before has all but disappeared.

Fear and doubt have been replaced with calm. "If this young man thinks he can do this," they say to themselves, "why can't I?"

Rudy brings hope, and they bring undying support.

And at the end of the day? They will all be Ironmen.

CHANGING A NATION FOREVER

His name is Emmanuel Ofosu Yeboah from Ghana. He was born with a birth defect: The lower part of his right leg dangled behind his right knee, which made it useless from day one. In his country, anyone with a disability is considered cursed, a second class citizen. Emmanuel's father was there at birth and, when he saw the deformity, deserted the family forever. Emmanuel's mother, Comfort, was told to abandon Emmanuel in the jungle like other parents of disabled children had done before her. She refused. Instead, she raised him like any other child and, when he was old enough, she carried young Emmanuel to school each morning. He was the only child with a disability in his school.

When Emmanuel was just 13 years old, his mother became ill, and Emmanuel left school to help support the family. Instead of resorting to begging – which is considered a way of life in Ghana for the disabled – Emmanuel opened a shoe-shine stand and brought in two to three dollars a day.

When he turned 18, his mother passed away. Emmanuel felt he needed to do something to honor her memory. After hearing about the Challenged Athletes Foundation (CAF) from a missionary, he sent a type-written grant request to the United States asking not for personal help but for a bicycle. He asked for a bicycle because he wanted to ride across his country to show the people that someone with a disability could do anything, that he and everyone like him had value.

CAF sent Emmanuel a bicycle and his world – and the world of the disabled in Ghana – changed forever.

Emmanuel Ofosu Yeboah rode 600 kilometers across his country with one leg on a mountain bike, and the nation was mesmerized. He was a combination of Martin Luther King and Forrest Gump. Kids ran after him chanting his name as he rode from village to village, and the print, radio and television media took notice that one of the two million disabled people in Ghana – 10 percent of the population – was finally standing up to make a difference.

In November of 2002, he was brought to California by CAF to participate in the San Diego Triathlon Challenge in La Jolla. He had never been out of Ghana and had never flown on an airplane. He arrived in this country with a grand total of three dollars in his pocket.

Emmanuel then completed the 56-mile bike ride in a little over seven hours with one leg, on a mountain bike. "I did not realize San Diego was so hilly," he joked afterwards.

His life has been a whirlwind ever since.

The folks from Loma Linda Hospital and Rehabilitation in Riverside, California, the title sponsors of the San Diego Triathlon Challenge, felt Emmanuel was a candidate for a prosthetic. Loma Linda agreed to handle the operation and take care of a home-stay. CAF provided the leg and round trip travel from Ghana to the United States and back.

In April of 2003, when Emmanuel arrived back in Los Angeles to have the operation, there was a surprise waiting for him. I had called Lisa Lax, the wonderfully talented producer who had garnered 13 Emmy awards for her work on both the Ironman World Championship television shows as well as the Olympics. She had left NBC and, with her twin sister Nancy Stern, was now creating documentary films with their company, Lookalike Productions.

"How about this for a documentary?" I asked. "Why not cover this young man from the moment he gets to Los Angeles and be there when he meets his home-stay, be there when he meets with his doctors, be there when his leg is amputated, be there when he takes his first step and be there when he does the San Diego Triathlon Challenge bike ride in November of 2003 with two legs rather than one?"

She agreed, and Lax and Stern have covered Emmanuel's journey ever since. The film *Emmanuel's Gift*, an 80-minute documentary narrated by Oprah Winfrey, was released in 2005.

The film captures Emmanuel taking his first step, then participating in a triathlon at Loma Linda that included a three-mile run and nine-mile bike ride less than two months after the operation. He then tagged off to double above-knee amputee swim stud Rudy Garcia-Tolson for the 100-yard swim.

When Emmanuel returned to Ghana, the film crew was there. Because his deformed leg had been removed, for the first time in his life Emmanuel wore long pants and was without crutches. He bounded off the plane into the arms of ecstatic family members.

He returned to the United States in November of 2003 and completed the San Diego Triathlon Challenge's 56-mile bike ride in four hours with two legs rather than one. He was honored as CAF's most inspirational athlete that afternoon and received his award from Academy Award winner Robin Williams. The next morning, he was on a flight to New York City where he had a meeting with fellow Ghanaian Kofi Annan, the secretary general of the United Nations, to discuss the rights of the disabled in Ghana. The following day, he was on a flight to Portland, Oregon to receive the Casey Martin Award on the Nike Campus in a packed auditorium. Along with that award came a $25,000 grant that CAF matched to help support Emmanuel's mission in Ghana and to have him represent CAF as an ambassador.

The disabled and their families are cursed. That was the belief in Ghana, and that's why no disabled person had ever been allowed inside the King's Palace. How much has Emmanuel changed the perception of the disabled in his country? In March 2005, five high-end wheelchairs along with 15 educational grants to disabled children, courtesy of CAF, were distributed in Ghana – at the King's Palace with a smiling king in attendance.

It all started so simply, with a young man hoping and dreaming for a new bike. It has evolved over time into a young man, with a little help from his friends, helping a nation to change forever.

Editor's Note: *For an update on Emmanuel Ofosu Yeboah and to learn about his foundation, go to www.emmanuelsdream.org. Its mission: to change society by empowering people with disabilities.*

ONE-ARM WILLIE

The date was November 5, 2006. Willie Stewart was 23 miles into the New York City Marathon and hating life. Every part of his body was screaming in anger after he had attacked the first half of the race like a man with a plane to catch. The wheels had not only come off the Stewart Express, he was now running on the rims and dragging those puppies along the pavement. The goal had been to run a fast one here in New York, but right now all he wanted to do was finish the darn thing before the sag wagon scooped his sorry butt off the road.

He was at 19 minutes for 5K, 37:44 for 10K and 1:21 at the half. Okay, you're right. This is nothing new. Stewart's PR (Personal Record) for the marathon is 2:42 and he has won the Catalina Marathon. He has also paddled the Grand Canyon and has spent 24 hours in a freezer, riding a Spin bike with another wacko named Antarctic Mike. Stewart tends to live his entire life with that fast-forward button on his personal remote pushed all the way to the floor.

Then it happened.

"I'm staggering along and all of a sudden I hear this motorcycle horn behind me," recalls Stewart. "I'm thinking, 'What the hell is a motorcycle doing in this mosh pit right now?' Then someone yells, 'Out of the way! Lance Armstrong is coming through!' My first thought was 'I can't let Lance beat me!'"

Armstrong, along with his own peloton, was in New York City for his first-ever marathon attempt. Running legends Joan Benoit and Alberto Salazar were serving as his domestiques, carrying his water and gel while the motorcycle clears the lesser-knowns out of his path. And while Stewart and the other 38,000 huddled masses were braving 40-degree temperatures for three-and-a-half hours before the race, Armstrong and the rest of the invitees were kept in warm seclusion, waiting to be led to the front of the group a few minutes before tip-off.

To get a sense of our man Willie's current plight, we need to take a quick trip in the Way Back Machine to get a snapshot of the weeks leading up to his current late-race crisis:

October 21: Stewart goes 11:16 at the Ford Ironman World Championship in Kona, Hawaii. Not bad for a guy with one arm. Try going 1:27 for a 2.4-mile swim with one arm tied behind your back and then 6:03 for the bike and 3:40 for the marathon.

October 28: After driving from Redlands to San Francisco the day before, Stewart rode the 86-mile first stage of the Qualcomm Million Dollar Challenge Bike Ride from San Francisco to Santa Cruz. Then he drove from Santa Cruz back to Redlands and the next day flew to Boston to be part of an experiment. ("*Nature* magazine is covering an anthropology study that is trying to prove that man is meant to run, not walk," says Stewart.)

November 1: To prove their theory, they are testing out runners, and Stewart committed to putting in three hours for them – on a treadmill . . . at race pace . . . four days before the marathon.

"I'm not always the brightest bulb in the building," laughs Stewart.

Now he was three miles from the finish of this bloody marathon, running on fumes with Armstrong breathing down his neck.

"My first thought was, 'What am I, chopped liver?'" says Stewart. "If Lance was going to get me he was going to have to earn it."

At 30 kilometers, Stewart had a six-minute gap on Armstrong. By 35 kilometers it was down to a little over a minute and a half. Even though his legs were screaming, Stewart wasn't about to concede.

"If it wasn't for Lance," he continues, "there is no way I would have gone under three hours."

Take that, yellow jersey guy. One-Arm Willie Stewart 2:59:03. Lance Armstrong 2:59:36. And if I'm not mistaken, I don't think Mr. Armstrong was racing Ironman two weeks earlier.

While Willie Stewart was proving once again that sports are the great equalizer, 3,000 miles away that same Sunday morning, 110 athletes with missing limbs or in wheelchairs were being introduced as the stars of the day at the San Diego Triathlon Challenge, the largest fundraiser for the Challenged Athletes Foundation.

In an interview a few years ago, I asked Stewart why he does what he does. He didn't hesitate.

"Sport makes me whole," he insisted. "When I'm racing, I'm the same as everyone else out there."

Not just the same, Willie. Sometimes even better.

FLAMINGO TIME

It didn't take him long to figure it out. Tom Sullivan, blind from birth, could hear the murmurs and chuckles as we walked our bike toward transition. The two of us were doing our first triathlon together and my primary responsibility, besides making sure we didn't swim, run or ride into any solid objects, was to secure a tandem.

Tom – the blind guy who as a golfer shoots in the 80s, had a movie made about his life called *If You Can See What I Hear*, had been a correspondent for ABC's *Good Morning America*, sang the national anthem at the Super Bowl, is a sought-after motivational speaker and has completed numerous marathons – would be riding on the back. The sighted guy, whose one claim to fame is that he has been in the sport of triathlon since 1978, has never, ever improved and had to scramble at the very last minute to actually find a tandem, is me. I would be on the front.

The bike was a 60-pound monstrosity that was coated with rust from top tube to spokes. The tires were cracked, bald and older than both of us put together. Oh yeah, did I mention that it had a pink plastic flamingo mounted on the front?

Which was why people were pointing and laughing.

"Babbitt, is there a pink flamingo on the front of this thing?" asked Mr. Observant as two friends and I struggled to lift the front wheel high enough to get it onto the rack.

"Why, yes, Tommy there is," I responded ever so casually. "Doesn't everyone have one?"

"That's awesome," screamed the always upbeat Tom. "I have never had a seeing eye flamingo before!"

As we passed people during the bike (yep, once we got up to speed, that 60-pound hulk could really motor) he kept yelling, "flamingo power!"

I have learned so many lessons from Tommy over the years. A few months after the triathlon, we were on a much-improved tandem, riding 75 miles in Colorado. I, of course, had no idea where we were since I am directionally challenged. Fortunately the blind guy on the back did. "You'll hit some gravel in a little bit," he said. "Take a left at the next street. "

He was spot on. The only limits we have, Tommy will tell you, are the ones we place on ourselves.

We sat down at a local hamburger joint after finishing that first triathlon. Still jazzed from our 3-mile run, 12-mile bike and 300-yard swim without falling down or taking someone out with our battering ram of a bike, I asked Tommy about growing up blind.

"In my entire life I have never met an ugly person," he said, laughing. He spoke about golf, his days as a wrestler plus acting, writing and singing. His life was exciting, and he loved it all.

As he continued, I finished my burger and fries but was still hungry. I asked him about the worst part about growing up blind and grabbed a few fries off his tray. Hey, they were sitting right there and the guy was blind, right? He'd never miss 'em.

Tommy had a very serious look on his face. "The worst part about growing up blind," he said softly, "is dealing with jerks who steal your fries."

These particular fries were three inches from my stealing-from-a-blind-guy lips when he exploded in laughter.

"Gotcha!" he screamed. "That's payback for putting me on that flamingo bike, Babbitt."

Blind? I guess it depends on how you define the term.

40 DIAPERS A DAY

Vanessa Tull, 38, of Thousand Oaks, California, is struggling up a hill near her home, but you wouldn't know it from the huge smile on her face. She is out training for 2006 The City of Los Angeles Marathon, her very first attempt at the distance. To Tull, the sun feels wonderful and there is nothing better than being outside in the fresh air. The key word here is "outside."

While Tull was pregnant with quadruplets − yep, quadruplets − she had to spend the last two months of her pregnancy on bed rest.

"It was so hard mentally, emotionally and physically," says Tull. "I was going crazy. The inspiration hit me while I was lying there. I couldn't imagine running a marathon being any harder than this."

That's when the decision was made, and that is why Vanessa Tull is now out pushing a baby carriage – not a baby jogger – with her four babies and her 6-year-old up this nasty hill.

She was never a runner before, but she is becoming one now. That's what happens when you push 160 pounds of children along with a 40-pound carriage up a hill over and over again.

"My legs haven't looked like this since high school," she laughs. Schlepping 200 pounds will do that.

Her 6-year-old gets on the carriage when it's time to trek uphill.

"Mom, do you need me to get in so you can get your workout in?"

Tull sings songs to keep her little ones entertained. When the babies fling their water cups out of the carriage, Tull looks at this as just another workout opportunity.

"I do lunges every time a water cup comes flying out," she says. "But after the third toss, the cups go back in the bag."

Tull has six kids – three boys and three girls – ranging from 20 months to 11 years. The number of diapers has actually dropped dramatically since the quadruplets were newborns.

"We're down to 20 a day," she says. "For the first seven to eight months we were changing 40 diapers a day."

Then, of course, there was feeding the quads. It took 30 minutes to feed each baby, so that's a solid two hours straight. They each needed to be fed every three hours.

"We had people come in to help us out," recalls Tull. "We set up 24-hour shifts so that there was always someone awake in the house."

Tull is getting help with her marathon training after winning a scholarship to the LA Roadrunners Training Program. The legendary Rod Dixon and his team will be there to help get her through what many consider one of the tougher days in sport.

But excuse Mrs. Tull if she's a tad skeptical.

"Before the babies, the thought of running one mile gave me a stomachache," she says. "But after going through a quadruple pregnancy, it doesn't scare me. Marathon, schmarathon. I don't mean any disrespect to people who have run marathons. Will it be hard? Absolutely. Will I ache all over for a really long time? Definitely. But it doesn't scare me because I know I'll live through it."

She did more than live through it. She made her kids proud.

Vanessa Tull went from 40 diapers a day to 26.2 miles in a day by finishing her first City of Los Angeles Marathon on March 19, 2006, in 6:45:42 – almost seven hours without dealing with a dirty diaper.

MR. CLUTCH

It was the culmination of every early morning swim workout and every day he spent doing flip turns while submerged in chlorinated water. You may be on a team as a swimmer, but when it comes down to the facts of life, when the gun goes off and you fly off the blocks, it's all about you against yourself and the water. Jason Lezak was a focused swimmer come lately, someone who, even though he swam in high school, still played baseball, basketball, soccer and was a water polo All-American. In those days, he focused on the 200 and 500 freestyle before discovering his ability to sprint.

"I swam pretty good times in high school," he recalls, "but not fast enough to be recruited by the top schools. My fastest times came in May of my senior year when most of the recruiting had already been done, so I decided to swim at Santa Barbara."

When the 6-foot, 2-inch, 205-pound, 32-year-old flew off to Beijing in the summer of 2008, it was going to be Jason Lezak's third Olympic experience. He took home a silver medal from the 4x100-meter freestyle relay in 2000 in Sydney and a bronze in the same event in 2004 in Athens. But, even though fellow American Gary Hall called him a professional relay swimmer, Lezak knew that he also had what it took to bring home an individual medal.

In 2004 that's what he was expecting when he arrived in Athens. "I should have been on the podium," he admits, "but I made a huge mistake, took the preliminaries too lightly and didn't even make it to the semifinals of the 100. I knew I had it in me, so I stuck it out until 2008 to give it another try." The hard part? Pieter van den Hoogenband, who took home the gold medal in 2004, swam the exact same time as Lezak did four weeks earlier in the Olympic Trials. "That was pretty tough," he admits.

In 2000 Gary Hall lit a fire under the Aussies in Sydney by saying the Americans would smash them like guitars in the finals of the 4x100. Guess again, Gary. The Aussies beat the Americans and then did a little air guitar concert on the pool deck to rub the Americans face in it a bit more.

Leading into the 4x100-meter relay finals in 2008, it was World Record Holder Alain Bernard of France who smacked the Americans before the race. He guaranteed the French would smash the Americans.

When Lezak left the blocks for the anchor leg on August 11, Bernard looked to be a man of his word. This is a guy who set three world records in one week that summer at the European Championships in the Netherlands, two at 100 meters and one at 50 meters. He was nicknamed the hovercraft because he appears to actually swim above the surface of the pool. Lezak was a full body length behind when he hit the water and the announcers had already conceded the win: "I don't believe they can do it. Bernard is pulling away and the Americans are trying to hang on to second."

Lezak didn't disagree. "I actually thought for a few seconds that there was no way I could catch this guy. He's the world record holder, and I don't stand a chance."

For the first 50 meters, Lezak, who breathes to the right, was flying blind. "I really didn't see Bernard until the turn," he says. "If I tried to look to my left to see where he was, it would take me out of my body alignment and ruin my stroke. By the time I got to the wall, I knew I would see him coming back."

But Lezak was gaining on every stroke. "Obviously I kept positive thoughts even though I had some negative thoughts go through me. I could see he was getting tired, and I was feeling pretty strong." With 15 meters to go, Lezak was closing fast as Bernard struggled. "I had so much adrenaline going I didn't feel a thing," recalls Lezak.

Jason Lezak came from a full body length behind to beat the world record holder in his event by swimming 46:06, the fastest relay leg in the history of swimming.

When he touched the wall, the whole world changed. By .08 of a second, he had turned defeat into victory, kept Michael Phelps quest for eight gold medals alive, inspired all of America and smacked down a smack-talking Frenchman.

What could be better than that?

"Being a big basketball fan, to look up and see Kobe Bryant and LeBron James standing up and pumping their fists in the air for us was pretty special, "says Lezak.

Lezak has watched the finish of the 4x100-freestyle relay more times than he cares to remember. He left Beijing with a total of six relay medals in his career and one individual medal, a bronze in the 100-meter freestyle in Beijing.

The individual medal was sweet, and Lezak is planning to stay in the pool and, hopefully, add to his personal medal count in 2012 in London. While the smack talk certainly helped fuel the fire, the desire to bring the 4x100-meter freestyle relay gold medal back home was a pretty important motivator as well.

"The motivation for me was being part of those relay teams in 2000 and 2004 where I felt we should have won – and being able to bring the title back to the United States where it belongs," says Lezak.

People talk about great clutch performances: John Elway leading the Broncos to win after win in the last two minutes of a game or Michael Jordan hitting the biggest shots when the game was on the line. It's time to add to that list the oldest member of the men's U.S Olympic swimming team in Beijing, Jason Lezak, swimming's Mr. Clutch.

Editors Note: *Jason Lezak qualified for his fourth Olympics at the 2012 United States Olympic Trials in Omaha, Nebraska. His sixth-place finish in the Olympic Trial finals was good enough to reach the London Games as a member of the U.S. 4x100-meter freestyle relay team. At the Olympics in London, Jimmy*

Feigen, Matt Grevers, Ricky Berens and Lezak swam for the U.S. team in the preliminaries. Nathan Adrian, Michael Phelps, Cullen Jones and Ryan Lochte swam in the finals, and together all these competitors earned a silver medal for the team's second-place finish in the finals.

LIVING THE DREAM

He was on the career track and never wavered. He went from high school to a college degree in economics and then on to graduate school for accounting. Growing up, education was everything in his household, and he had made his mom and dad proud.

"In our home, it was always education first, sports second," he says. "Participating in athletics was something for the weekends."

He was 23 years old and had a great job. He owned two suits and a collection of dress shirts and ties. He rode the train to work every day, caught up on the financial news daily and received a nice pay check every Thursday – plus he had an amazing view from his office of the city's skyline.

And he hated every second of every day.

"I had been at my job for 10 months, and I'd look out of my window and daydream about riding and swimming and running," he recalls. "I probably wasn't a very productive accountant."

He had been successful as an age-group triathlete, but what if he could quit his job and travel the world and race as a professional triathlete?

One day he went in and told his boss he was quitting. "My boss thought I had another job offer. He laughed when I told him that no, I was leaving to become a professional triathlete. He thought that was hilarious."

But how to break the news to the folks? That was going to be a tough one.

"For two weeks I would get up in the morning, put on my suit and tie, and my dad would drop me off at the train station," he recalls. "Then I would get off at the first stop, go home and spend the day on my bike."

Eventually, though, he knew he would have to face the music. When he finally sat down with his parents to tell them the news, his mom was supportive but his dad was silent. "That was the worst," he says. "I would much rather have him be angry and yell at me. When he went quiet, I said 'Dad, don't be disappointed, be angry.'"

It turns out his dad was just processing the information. His dad's response was something the son would remember forever.

"He said, 'Son, if this is what you want to do, if you want to be a professional athlete . . . than BE a professional athlete. Don't waste the next 10 years of your life being stupid. Do it properly. If you become the best you can be, I will be very proud of you.'"

So he bought an open-ended ticket to Europe, flew to Paris with $2,700 in his pocket and bought a triathlon magazine when he landed.

"I stayed in these cheap hotels I booked through Hotel Formule 1 [a low-budget European hotel chain] and raced three times every weekend. I was going to race until I either made it or ran out of money," he laughs.

In Orange, France, he paid up front for a hotel for three nights and ended up staying five. "The hotel manager kept coming up to my room looking for the money for the fourth and fifth nights," he recalls. "I ended up climbing out the window and bailing on paying for the last two nights. She's probably still looking for me."

Triathlon is a little different in Europe. He might have a smaller event on Friday afternoon and a bigger one on Saturday in the same city in France. Then he would hop the slow train Saturday night so that he could avoid paying for a hotel night, arrive in Switzerland in the morning and then race Sunday.

"One weekend I made $1,000 and thought I was the richest guy in the world, that I'd never have to work again," he says. "I was amazed and thrilled by it all. I wanted to prove to my mom and dad that I did do it properly, that I had made the right decision."

That decision led him to winning the 1997 ITU World Triathlon Championship, Wildflower, Escape from Alcatraz, Chicago International Triathlon, St. Croix, Ironman Australia and the 2007 and 2010 Ford Ironman World Championship titles.

Do dreams come true?

Ask Chris McCormack.

Johan Otter

MIRACLES

TAZ THE WONDER DOG

RAISIN' THE BAR

THE DEFENDER

CHAPTER 7 – MIRACLES

"I wanted so badly to live. I wasn't ready to die. I thought about my life, my family and my friends and how much they meant to me. I wanted to tell them all how much I loved them.
Those thoughts were so strong I didn't really feel pain when I was lying there.
All I wanted to do was survive."

– Danelle Ballengee

TAZ THE WONDER DOG

What do you do now, Danelle? That had to be the question rampaging through her mind.

Forget winning the Eco Challenge and Primal Quest multi-day adventure races. Or climbing all 54 of Colorado's 14,000-foot peaks in 14 days and change. Or the seven Ironman finishes, along with the world mountain running championships and the six U.S. Athlete of the Year awards in four different sports. This was a new sport, one that she had never hoped to participate in: It's called survival.

It was December 13, 2006 and Danelle Ballengee was playing back the last few hours in her mind. It had started like so many other workouts. She parked her truck at the trailhead a few miles from her home in Moab, Utah, put on running shoes, grabbed Taz, her mixed breed that she has had for three years – since he was only 7 weeks old – and headed out for a two-hour jog. A romp up a jeep road to the canyon followed by a short scramble up the rocks to another jeep road. It was on the short scramble where her life turned upside down. Ballengee hit some black ice and her feet went out from under her as she slid down the face of the rock. For an athlete who is always in control, this had to be the worst possible scenario. She was sliding to oblivion and there was absolutely nothing she could do about it. She flew past an overhang and plunged 60 feet to a rock shelf.

"I thought I was dead," Ballengee admits. "I reached down to touch my legs to see if I was paralyzed or not." She wasn't. But her pelvis was rotated and fractured on both sides, there were fractures in three of her vertebrae and her sacrum was split down the middle.

With the adrenaline still flowing, Ballengee was somehow able to crawl a quarter-mile as she tried to get out of the canyon before sunset. It took her a full five hours to negotiate that quarter-mile. Remember, this is Moab in December. The forecast was for temperatures to dip into the low 20s overnight. Ballengee was wearing baggy running tights, a thin base layer, a polypro shirt and a thin fleece over the top. She also had a fleece hat and gloves plus a shower cap that she happened to have with her. A shower cap?

"We use them all the time in adventure racing," says Ballengee. "You put it over your hat to keep in the heat."

Ballengee was lucky. The shower cap just happened to be in her water bottle holder, left over from a previous race. She had made it to a pothole and broke a hole in it with her bottle to get water.

"By this time it was 5 p.m., and I realized I was stuck there," she says. "I stayed up all night, rubbing my hands, tapping my feet and doing crunches. Taz curled up with me to try and keep me warm."

Not having anyone to talk to, her conversations through day two were with Taz.

"I told him that I was hurt, that maybe he could get some help," she recalls. "I think that dogs are a lot smarter than we realize."

Before going out for her run, Ballengee didn't leave a note or call anyone. She realized that there was a good chance no one even knew she was in danger. As the second night approached, Ballengee's neighbor, Dorothy Rosignol, realized that something was wrong. The lights and computer were on at Ballengee's house and the blinds were wide open. After a call to her parents, search and rescue went into action, and by dawn of day three they had started to hunt for Ballengee.

If she tried to move, the pain was excruciating. So she stayed as still as possible and thought about simply staying alive.

"I wanted so badly to live. I wasn't ready to die. I thought about my life, my family and my friends and how much they meant to me. I wanted to tell them all how much I loved them. Those thoughts were so strong I didn't really feel pain when I was lying there. All I wanted to do was survive," says Ballengee.

By day three, Taz realized that something was seriously wrong. His owner had never stayed in one spot for so long, and he hadn't had anything to eat.

"Taz took off several times. I finally realized that he was running all the way to the trailhead and back hoping to find help," recalls Ballengee. "It was five miles or so each way. Taz would run to the trailhead, look for help, then run back and lick me in the face before heading off on another run. He did this even though he hadn't had food in three days."

On what was to be his last run, Taz arrived at the trailhead at noon, just as the search and rescue team found Ballengee's truck. At first they didn't know that this crazy dog running around biting and barking was Taz. They were thinking about taking him to animal control before they realized that this was Ballengee's dog. They got on their all-terrain vehicles and followed Taz, who did a Lassie and took them right to Ballengee. By this time, she had lost a third of her blood. Most people can live 8-12 hours after sustaining similar injuries with that much blood loss. The doctors told Ballengee that she was lucky to be alive, that she was only able to withstand 56 hours of torture because of her amazing level of fitness.

That night, the temperatures dropped into the teens and it snowed.

"I don't think I would have made it through another night," says Ballengee softly. "I am just so lucky."

Lucky to be alive and lucky to have a friend like Taz.

Ballengee was interviewed by the *Today* show while in her hospital bed. At the end of the interview she was reunited with Taz The Wonder Dog. It was an emotional scene.

Being right before Christmas, Ballengee was asked if she was going to put an extra bone in Taz's stocking.

"A bone?" she laughed as she petted Taz. "He'll be getting steak!"

A few days later, a large box arrived from Michigan. When Ballengee opened the box, she found a Christmas Stocking with Taz's name embroidered on it. Underneath? A six-pack of steaks for the hero of the day.

Sometimes it's all about payback. When Taz was a puppy, Ballengee adopted him from puppy rescue in Boulder, Colorado.

Three years later, Taz repaid the favor.

Editor's Note: *Since the accident, Danelle Ballengee has become a mother of two boys, Noah and William. She also owns and operates Milt's Stop N' Eat Diner in Moab, Utah and puts on a trail marathon that actually traverses the spot where she nearly died. That area is now called, fittingly enough, Taz's Canyon.*

RAISIN' THE BAR

It was a Raisin family tradition that started when Saul was a boy. If his parents, Jim and Yvonne, squeezed his hand three times, it meant *I love you*, one squeeze for each word. Saul didn't have to say a word. To respond he would squeeze four times, *I love you too*, and the message was sent.

On April 4, 2006, the now 23-year-old pro cyclist from Dalton, Georgia, was fighting for his life. Saul Raisin from Team Credit Agricole, who had been named the "best young rider" at the Tour of Georgia, won a stage at Le Tour de Langkawi and took home the King of the Mountains jersey at the Tour de l'Avenir, had crashed during the Circuit de la Sarthe that day in France. Raisin went down on a patch of gravel and broke his collarbone and scapula. He also landed on his head.

Raisin always texted his mom "I'm okay" after each race. When the text didn't arrive, she had one of those maternal premonitions that something was very wrong. When team director Roger Legeay called the Raisins, he told Yvonne and Jim that their son had crashed but he would be okay.

That was before the doctors realized that Raisin was bleeding into his brain.

Legeay called the family's home 30 hours later, but this time the message was much worse. "My parents were told that doctors had to perform emergency surgery," says Raisin. "I would be put into a medically induced coma, and I probably wouldn't be alive by the time they got to France."

The impact of the accident left a hole in the right side of Raisin's brain and, if he lived, he would most likely be paralyzed on the left side of his body. "My parents were told that they should think about donating my organs," he says.

Six days after the coma was induced, Raisin started to emerge from the fog. "My dad came to the right side of the hospital bed, and my mom was on my left," he recalls. "My dad grabbed my right hand and whispered in my ear *Daddy loves you* and squeezed three times. I squeezed four times: *I love you too.* Then my mom did the same thing on the left side, the side that was supposed to be paralyzed forever, and I squeezed four times again."

The nurse insisted it was impossible for him to be doing this after brain surgery and after being in a coma. "Then I squeezed her hand four times, and she started screaming, 'It's a miracle!'" says Raisin.

It took a month before Raisin put the puzzle pieces together. He remembered nothing from the crash. When he was able to check his e-mail, there were 1,200 get-well notes from everyone from George Hincapie to Lance Armstrong. When he went to Google, there were 550,000 search results. "I couldn't understand what was happening," he admits. "I thought maybe I had won the Giro d'Italia."

Five years after the crash, Saul Raisin, who was told he would never walk again, has become a runner, completing the New York City and Atlanta Marathons. He is also a triathlete, completing 70.3 Timberman, 70.3 Steelhead, 70.3 New Orleans, the Wildflower Long Course, and the Ironman World Championship 70.3 in Las Vegas. The charity he created, Raisin Hope (www.saulraisin.com), is dedicated to helping people with traumatic brain injuries.

"I can do more now for others than I could ever have done as a pro cyclist," he insists. "I have been given a second chance at life, and I plan to make the most of it."

THE DEFENDER

It was August 25, 2005 and Johan and Jenna Otter, 43-year-old father and his 18-year-old daughter, were out for a hike in Montana's Glacier National Park. The two were 90 minutes into a six-hour hike when they came around a corner and ran smack dab into hell.

A 350-pound grizzly bear was five feet away with two of her cubs. The bear and Johan Otter were kindred spirits, both taken by surprise, both wanting nothing else but to protect their own.

Otter put himself between the bear and Jenna and it was on. "The bear bit down on my left thigh and wasn't about to let go," he recalls. "It wasn't very pleasant."

Otter remembers being shaken around like a rag doll.

"If you are attacked by a bear, you're supposed to get into the fetal position to protect your front side and play dead," he says. Fat chance. The bear already had him by the front side, and he was at the worst spot on the trail to be attacked. The only escape from the dental floss thin trail was a cliff with a sheer drop off.

Options? He didn't have many. The bear was inflicting major damage, breaking seven vertebrae in Otter's neck and back, one in five places. His right eye socket was crushed, and he had numerous puncture wounds and three broken ribs. His scalp was torn nearly completely off and he was on his way to losing 50 percent of the blood in his body. "If I stayed there, I was going to die," says Otter.

To stay alive and to keep the bear away from Jenna, he dove 25 feet off the cliff while grabbing the bear by the throat. The two landed amidst the hard scrabble and continued their battle. Otter seized a rock and repeatedly beat the bear in the head. He knew he was in bad shape when he could actually feel the bear's teeth going into his skull. The two tumbled another 50 feet – 75 feet total – down the side of the mountain.

Time was crawling. Johan Otter's life had been altered forever in the span of what turned out to be five minutes. "I wasn't afraid at all," he insists. "I just knew I had to keep the bear with me."

The bear finally left him, and he yelled to see if Jenna was okay. It turned out that Jenna had played dead and been scratched on the right cheek, but then the bear and her cubs had disappeared. When Jenna finally saw her dad again, he was coated with blood and crawling towards her.

The two screamed for help for an hour before some hikers heard them. It took two hours from the time of the attack for the rangers to get there and four more hours for a helicopter to arrive. By that time, the paramedics could barely find Otter's pulse.

They strapped him down and, with Otter dangling 30-40 feet below the chopper, flew him out.

"After they landed, they asked if it was okay to go back and pick up my daughter before heading off to the hospital," he laughs. Since his one-on-one battle with the bear was all about keeping Jenna out of harm's way, there was no way he was going anywhere without her by his side.

Being a physical therapist himself, he avoided having his spine fused and instead sported a halo for three months.

"The minute they told me I had a broken neck, I told them no fusion," he says. "They couldn't convince me otherwise and, quite frankly, I was in such bad medical shape I really wasn't a candidate at that point. It took eight hours of surgery just to clean me up."

Johan Otter is a long-time marathon runner. His first was the inaugural Rock 'N' Roll Marathon in San Diego in 1998, and his personal best is 3:14:05. He knows that the fitness that he accumulated from his running passion saved his life. So it was not surprising that in June of 2006 he would try to keep his streak alive at the Rock N Roll Marathon in San Diego. He had run the first eight events, so why not number nine?

"The first time I tried to run after getting the halo off, I had to stop after about 10 minutes," he recalls. "It was a total bummer."

Ten months after the attack, Otter ran 3:39 – and was disappointed.

This is from a guy who had   most of his scalp destroyed by the bear. The doctors took skin and muscle from other parts of his body and are still working on rebuilding the top of his head.

But what's inside seems damn near indestructible. In late July 2006, Otter went back to Montana to finish what he started on August 25, 2005: the hike to the Grinnell Glacier. While Jenna wasn't interested in getting back on the trail, for psychological cleansing, Otter knew he had to complete the trek.

When you are out hiking in bear country, you are taught to carry bear spray and to yodel so that you don't ever catch a bear by surprise. Not that it would have mattered, but Otter's bear spray was in his pack during that first hike and not on his belt where he knew it should have been. And he hadn't been very good about yodeling either.

But for the return engagement, on the trail he was a yodeling fool. "I yodeled all the way up," he insists.

He did the hike with his wife, and the 10-mile round trip with 1,600 feet of climbing took around seven hours.

"It was a really emotional experience," he says. "When my face was coated with blood and I wasn't sure if I was blind, the first thing I saw out of my right eye was Glacier Lake. That was right before I jumped off the cliff and into the bush. To see the lake again made me feel at home."

He also saw a few bears from a distance during that second trip. "I thought to myself, 'you're an amazing animal, but you're not that good looking up close.'"

Does he harbor any anger?

No way. He totally understands. "She did exactly what she was supposed to do," he insists. "She was protecting her family."

David Goggins

MILITARY HEROES

A SALUTE TO HIS SOLDIERS

A WARRIOR FOR THE FALLEN

BOOTS AND UTES

"DON'T EVER GIVE UP"

A BLESSING

CHAPTER 8 – MILITARY HEROES

"Brave. Rifles. Veterans. During the Mexican wars, General Scott said those three words to his men after their first major victory. It means that we have been baptized in blood and fire and come out as steel. It is an expression that I live by. I am stronger and more powerful because of what I have gone through."

– Lt. Col. David Rozelle

A SALUTE TO HIS SOLDIERS

It was June 21, 2003, a typical steamy day in Hit (pronounced Heat), Iraq, as Capt. David Rozelle got into his Humvee to lead his men out on a mission. He had been told earlier that week by the local leaders that, because he had helped to shut down the black market in guns, ammunition and gas, there was now a price on his head – $1,000 to the person who takes him out. He was warned to not join his men when they went out on patrol. "Your men will be safe, but you will be attacked."

Not going with his men was never an option for Rozelle, a man who feels that a real leader leads from the front.

"There was no way I would ever stay behind," he says. "What type of message does that send to your men?"

Not far into the mission, his Humvee drove over an anti-tank land mine, lifting it off the ground and blowing the front end apart. The 100-pound right tire and wheel landed 100 meters away. Rozelle, who was sitting right above where the explosion was centered, was bleeding profusely from his arms, legs and face. Two of his men ran to him and evacuated him from the scene. Within two hours, Rozelle was in a hospital outside of Baghdad where the doctor gave him two options.

"He told me that there were no muscles, tendons or ligaments left to support the lower part of my right leg," recalls Rozelle. "He told me he could try to save the lower leg but that I'd have a club foot that would be worthless and eventually I'd want to have it removed."

He laughs. "That was actually an option he gave me. The other was that he would save as much of the leg as he could, amputate the rest, and I would be back running on a prosthetic within a year."

After making option two a reality, Rozelle was flown to Walter Reed Army hospital in Washington, D.C. where the 220-pound former rugby player now weighed a paltry 170. When his mom walked into the room, they both hugged and cried. Then she brought up an incident that occurred at a running race when he was younger.

"My mom reminded me that I was really hurting and that she came up to me with about two miles to go and told me that she was going to run with me and finish together," recalls Rozelle. "Then she told me, 'I'm here now and we're going to do it again. I'll be with you the whole way.'"

Rozelle ended up back home in Fort Collins, Colorado, trying to deal with life as an amputee. It was a struggle. To deal with the real pain and the phantom pain that goes with limb loss – non-existent toes itching, cramps in a calf muscle that is no longer there – Rozelle did everything he could to make the pain disappear.

"We're human and sometimes we're weak," admits Rozelle. Morphine made the pain go away, so he would set his alarm to get his fix every two hours. When he wasn't on morphine, whisky was his self-medication of choice.

"I wasn't a good husband or a good father," he continues. "I stayed up late, woke up late and watched television all day. I couldn't even drive."

Then a letter arrived that changed everything. It was the last letter he wrote to his wife, Kim, from Iraq. At the time he wrote the letter, she was due to have their first child, Forrest, any day.

"When I read that letter, I realized the pain my wife would have felt if she had received it after I died," says Rozelle. "I knew I was in denial, that I was addicted to morphine and that my total focus was on myself."

He eliminated morphine cold turkey, dealt with two horrendous weeks of withdrawal, and then found a new addiction. "I started working out 3-5 hours a day and then completed my first triathlon. There is no greater feeling in the world."

Rozelle went from one minute of jumping rope to 15 minutes. He learned to swim again and got on a mountain bike. He took indoor cycling classes and rode his bike to and from the gym. Then he did the Pueblo Triathlon on his walking foot and ended up on crutches for a few weeks as a result. But he didn't care. The weight was coming off, and he was once again the old David Rozelle.

In late October 2004, he did the 1.2-mile swim at the San Diego Triathlon Challenge. The next week, he ran the New York City Marathon. By Thanksgiving, he passed the physical to get back into active duty and resume his command in Iraq.

Go back? David, haven't you given enough?

"It's hard to explain the sense of duty I feel as an army officer," he says. "My obligation was to go back with my men. I was healed and ready to go emotionally and physically. I wanted to prove to my fellow soldiers that this was not going to bring me down, and I wanted to take back my life from exactly where I left it two years ago."

Brave. Rifles. Veterans. Those are words Rozelle used with his men often.

"During the Mexican wars," he explains, "General Scott said those three words to his men after their first major victory. It means that we have been baptized in blood and fire and come out as steel. It is an expression that I live by. I am stronger and more powerful because of what I have gone through."

No other soldier who has lost a limb in battle had ever gone back to his command with a prosthetic. In March of 2005, Rozelle proved that he had indeed come out as steel by becoming the first. Then his focus shifted from steel to Iron.

When he returned to the states after his second tour of duty in early June 2005, the man, now Maj. Rozelle, began working with the soldiers at Walter Reed Army Hospital who came back from battle missing limbs or in a wheelchair. The program he spearheads for the Challenged Athletes Foundation (CAF) is called Operation Rebound.

In June 2006, Rozelle completed the Ford Ironman Coeur d'Alene in 13:55:01. At the finish line, he stood strong and saluted his soldiers.

"It was important for me to look strong and powerful coming across the line," says Rozelle. "My soldiers need to know that if I can do it so can they."

Editor's Note: *Maj. David Rozelle (now a lieutenant colonel) went on to finish the 2006 Ford Ironman World Championship and became the first war amputee to complete the grueling triathlon. For more about Operation Rebound, go to www.challengedathletes.org and click on "What We Do" and then "Operation Rebound."*

A WARRIOR FOR THE FALLEN

David Goggins – all 6-feet, 1-inch, 195 pounds of him – is a Navy SEAL who actually used to be a lot bigger. And he used to bench press a lot more.

"I used to bench press 435, but now I'm at 275 or so," says Goggins. Of course, the guy is 100 pounds – yep 100 pounds – lighter than he used to be.

"Lifting was a passion for me," he insists. "In my powerlifting days, I used to look at runners and cyclists like they weren't that tough. Now I realize how wrong I was. Going long distances is the only way to really test your soul."

Goggins is the type of guy who likes to see where the human limits are and then maybe push a few thousand miles beyond them. His first triathlon? Nope, not your garden variety half-mile swim, 12-mile bike ride and 5K run. When Goggins decides to dive into something, he dives deep. His first triathlon was an event in Kona, Hawaii, in November of 2006 called the Ultraman.

Day one is a 6.2-mile ocean swim and a tough 90-mile ride; day two is a brutal 171-mile bike ride (261 total cycling miles); and day three is a 52.4-mile run from Hawi, the bike turnaround at the Ironman World Championship, back to sleepy downtown Kailua Kona.

How did Mr. Goggins train for his first triathlon? Since, as a SEAL, he had to go to work early every day, he would be up and training at 3 a.m.

He borrowed a bike from a buddy; and starting about three weeks before race day, immediately ramped up his mileage to a cool 300 miles per week. Sort of like the guy in your physics class speed reading the textbook as the final exam is being passed out.

But unlike our physics flunkee-to-be, Goggins aced his exam, finishing second overall by a mere 10 minutes at the Ultraman.

"I lost over 30 minutes dealing with a flat tire on day two," he recalls. After he flatted, he used a rental bike that he had with him just in case. Unfortunately it didn't have clip-in pedals, so he rode the last 20 miles or so in his running shoes strapped into old-style cages.

In July 2006, Goggins ran the Kiehl's Badwater Ultramarathon – 135 miles across Death Valley in over 100-degree heat – and finished in fifth place overall. No 5Ks or 10Ks or marathons for David Goggins. Nope. His first-ever organized running event was a 24-hour race in San Diego, California, consisting of one-mile loops. Goggins had to run 100 miles in under 24 hours to qualify for Badwater. When he went through 101 miles in 18 hours and 56 minutes, he went home – mission accomplished.

So, David, you have transformed your body and you are now an endurance athlete. Are you into it for the runner's high or the glow of a great workout? How much do you love this?

Not much, says Goggins.

"I don't like any of this stuff," he insists. "My life is about doing things you don't like to do. I figure I can suffer through just about anything. I'm doing this to raise money for our Special Operations Warrior Foundation. All the money we raise goes to help out the kids of Special Operation Forces that lost their lives in the line of duty to go to college. So far, we have helped put 266 kids through college. That's my motivation. That's what keeps me going."

Don't look for David Goggins to come over to the dark side and start wearing a Speedo or shaving down anytime soon. "That won't be happening," he laughs. "There will be no Speedos worn by David Goggins and no shaving of any leg hair."

This is a man who obviously enjoys testing himself – a lot. But even Goggins has to come face to face with doubt when he is doing events that require suffering under extreme conditions for hours and days on end.

"When I start to question myself out there, I think back to when I quit or failed at something when I was younger," he admits. "If you are any kind of man or any kind of woman, you know you never want to feel that way again. My philosophy is that eventually the pain is going to end. Nothing lasts forever so you might as well dig down deep and get through it. Quitting is just not an option."

For more information on the Special Operations Warrior Foundation, go to www.specialops.org.

Editor's Note: *On January 20, 2013, David Goggins broke the world record for pull-ups in 24 hours when he completed 4,025 in 17 hours in Brentwood, Tennessee.*

BOOTS AND UTES

Officially the name is William Conner, and he is 35 years old and from Tulsa, Oklahoma. But it's okay, you can call him Bill or Wild Bill, he'll answer to either. On Ironman day 2008 in toasty Kona, Hawaii, he was the guy who obviously had not anted up for quality time in the wind tunnel before race day.

If he had, someone might have mentioned to him that the eight-pound combat helmet that was perched on his dome was probably not the most aerodynamic, lightweight or comfortable way to go. They might have noticed that the utilities and marine issue boots – also known as boots and utes – that he was wearing during the 112-mile ride probably were a tad much for the occasion. Who else takes their boots to their local bike shop to have them adapted so that Speedplay cleats could be mounted to the bottom?

"I was going to use cages and just slide my boots into those," recalls Conner. "But the guys at the bike shop thought they could make the Speedplay cleats and pedals work, and it definitely helped."

His feet did go numb for the last 20 miles of the bike ride, but he was in luck! He had another pair of exactly the same really heavy footwear waiting in his extra large transition bag so that he could run the marathon in those. With his feet now totally soaked with sweat, he could look forward to 26.2 miles of fun.

"By mile three I already had blisters on both feet," he recalls.

As you might have guessed, Wild Bill was on a bit of a mission. After four tours of duty in Iraq in 2004, 2005, 2006 and 2008 – and after finally being accepted through the lottery into the Ford Ironman World Championship after applying every year since 1996 – our young marine was going to make the most of his once-in-a-lifetime opportunity. He was in Fallujah when he received the news that he had been accepted, so he went into full on training mode. He had an indoor cycling bike in his office and lived in this 8-by-8-foot room for months as he prepared. On Saturday nights, he would do his long rides. From 5-7 p.m., he would ride his mountain bike around the perimeter of the base and then, after the sun went down, he would ride another four and a half hours on his indoor bike and create a river of sweat on the floor around him in the 90-degree room.

"It was like riding in a sauna," he says.

When he had first gone to Iraq in 2005, he ran three days in a row around the complex; but that ended abruptly when a rocket zoomed over his head.

"I thought maybe that was a sign that I better stop running for a while," he laughs.

On race day, the heat training he had been doing in Iraq came in handy. Despite the boots and helmet and fatigues, he felt downright cool.

"My transition times were pretty slow because I changed utility trousers, socks and boots after the bike ride," he says.

Racing for yourself in Kona is always special. But racing for someone else makes the day something you will never forget. Wild Bill dedicated the swim to Marine Major Doug Zenbiec, who died during an ambush in Baghdad. The bike ride was for Navy SEAL Lieutenant Commander Erik Kristensen, who died in Afghanistan; and the run was for Marine Major Megan McClung, who was killed in Iraq when an IED (improvised explosive device) exploded under the Humvee she was riding in.

We look at Ironman as a day of sport, a day of entertainment, a day of perseverance, a day of celebration and a day that proves to each of us how far the human body can be pushed.

For Second Lieutenant Marine Corporal Wild Bill Conner, he looked at Ironday as a way to honor three heroes and their families.

Boots and Utes were the perfect dress for the occasion.

"DON'T EVER GIVE UP"

The date was April 4, 2004. Camp Taji is located 30 miles north of Baghdad, Iraq. Army Major Anthony Smith, a former scholarship athlete at Alcorn State University in Lorman, Mississippi, in football, basketball and track, was part of the 1st Calvary Division, 39th Infantry Brigade Combat Team.

"We were a special operations group that made sure supplies were where they were supposed to be," Smith says.

Smith's unit was attacked, and he suffered a direct hit from an RPG, a Rocket Propelled Grenade. "It hit me on the right side of my body, and I ended up with a traumatic brain injury, blindness in my right eye, right kidney failure and hearing loss in my right ear. My jaw was broken in four places, and my nose was broken in two places. I lost my right arm, my right hip, half my femur, my quad and back muscles, the large intestine and part of my colon, and a portion of the back of my skull," he says.

At first they couldn't find Smith. He was listed as missing. When they did find him, his heart flat-lined. Check that. It flat-lined *three times*.

"They listed me as killed in action," he says calmly.

It obviously takes a lot more than a RPG to stop Smith. After being declared dead, he was placed in a body bag. When a nurse unzipped the bag to get his dog tags, Smith sat up.

"The nurse ran over to the doctor who told her, 'Well, bodies move sometimes'" Smith was told. "Then she told him that I was talking and asking for help."

Since he had been declared Killed in Action, Smith's records had been sent ahead and no one knew his blood type. They gave him B positive rather than B negative. He immediately went into shock, and doctors induced a coma that lasted 62 days.

Smith came out of the coma at Brooks Army Hospital in Texas.

"When I woke up, two nurses and a doctor were there. They didn't know I was awake. They said I would never walk, see or speak again and that someone was going to have to take care of me."

Anthony Smith had always been a man of faith.

"I think what separates me from other people is that I knew there had to be a reason I survived," he says.

Smith ballooned up to over 300 pounds and was smoking three packs of cigarettes a day while trying to figure out his purpose. Then he realized he wanted to be an athlete again and started with swimming and then began to ride a bike. He walked his first 5K in an hour and 36 minutes and later walked his second in just over 56 minutes.

In 2009, with a prosthetic arm, he rode 420 miles during a San Francisco to San Diego bike tour. "At 246 pounds, the Big Sur stage was tough for me, so I rode in a car that day," he admits.

But his heart is in martial arts. A man who was declared dead, who flat-lined three times and was in a body bag, now owns Anthony's Martial Arts Academy in his home of Blytheville, Arkansas.

"I have over 300 members now," he says proudly. "I love teaching kids."

While in the hospital, he remembers the doctors saying they were going to amputate his leg. His arm was already gone.

"I thought they had saved my arm," he recalls, "so I told them not to take my leg."

Actually, what they had saved was the *tattoo* that had been on his arm. They doctors cut off the arm below the tattoo and lifted the skin over the bone.

"So my tattoo stayed," Smith says with a smile.

The tattoo, written in Korean, perfectly sums up the man.

It says, "Don't ever give up."

A BLESSING

George Foster grew up in a depressed neighborhood in Baltimore. With no father in the home, his mother worked two jobs to support him and his three siblings.

"When my little sister was born she was sick, so my mom had to use her savings to pay the medical bills. When she couldn't pay the utility bills, we went without electricity and hot water most of that winter. All of us slept in one bed to stay warm."

As a boy, young Foster escaped from reality through his G.I. Joe action figures. "It was my dream," he says, "to grow up and become a real-life G.I. Joe."

Right out of high school in 1994, Foster enlisted in the Marines.

In 2002 he was sent to Iraq. Foster was 100 yards from his compound's front gate when a vehicle full of explosives detonated. Even at 220 pounds, the force of the blast threw him to the ground.

"I thought I was fine," he says, "but when I returned home, all I wanted to do was ride my motorcycle and be by myself." When he was coaching youth sports at the Miramar Marine Corps Air Station northeast of San Diego, everything was good. But when he put on the uniform and went to work, he was an angry guy.

"I had post-traumatic stress disorder (PTSD) but didn't realize it," he admits. "Someone would ask me a question, and I'd blow up. I had these anger spikes that I just couldn't control."

His next deployment was to Afghanistan in 2010. For more than three straight months, enemy forces would send rounds into the base at all times of the day and night.

"I stayed up for four straight days," Foster admits. "If I was awake, I was angry. The doctors gave me medication, but I was on an emotional roller coaster because of the combination of psychiatric medication. I had become suicidal. Every day I would sit at my desk and wonder, 'If I shot myself right now in the head, would that hurt more than shooting myself in the chest?' It's hard to explain to people, but it just hurt to be alive."

His therapist came up with an idea. She told him to put together a list of what he would like to do in his life just in case he decided not to kill himself.

"I sat down to make my list, and I remembered being a little boy watching Dave Scott and Mark Allen on TV doing the Ironman," he recalls. "I asked my mom if I could do that one day, and she told me that I could do anything I set my mind to. Triathlon went to the top of my list."

He taped up that list next to his bed and signed up for the 2011 Ironman 70.3 in Oceanside, California. He had a panic attack in the swim and was third to last out of the water.

"Twenty-six miles into the ride, I got off my bike and cried for about three minutes," he admits. "I didn't know if I could go on. 'Why the hell am I doing this?' I asked myself."

Then he thought of his mom, who had passed away six years earlier, and felt that she would be with him the rest of the way. He finished in 7:54. Mom was right. George Foster could do anything.

While triathlon will never replace medication and counseling, Foster feels that it is essential to his happiness.

"If I'm racing or volunteering, I'm constantly involved with great, positive people," he says. "You can't control the panic attacks from PTSD, but you can control how you deal with them. I have a purpose now, and that purpose is to keep moving forward. Triathlon has been a blessing."

Lt. Colonel David Rozelle finishing the 2006 Ironman World Championship

Dave Scott (left) and Mark Allen

LEGENDARY

"PRE" AND ROD

A TAINTED MEMORY

THE HOLY GRAIL

OUTKICKED BY A 14-YEAR-OLD

ONE AND DONE

MEANT TO BE

DAVE SCOTT'S SIGNATURE STYLE

PLAYING CATCH ON THE QUEEN K

WHY NOT DROP OUT?

CHICKEN SOUP AND A GLOW STICK

BULLY A BULLY

AN IRON GENT

THANKS FOR BELIEVING

CHAPTER 9 – LEGENDARY

"People said that Pre was arrogant. But remember, I lived with John Walker, who was pretty arrogant himself. Pre knew that if he had doubt, that the other guys in the field had it as well.
Pre didn't really have that killer instinct, but he knew what it took to be the best. He was never afraid of the pain. We played hard… but we trained harder."

– Legendary runner Rod Dixon on fellow legend Steve Prefontaine

"PRE" AND ROD

Their first meeting came after the 1972 Olympics. At those games in Munich, America's young gun, Steve Prefontaine, took fourth place in the Olympic 5000 meters while New Zealand's Rod Dixon took home a bronze in the 1500.

For the man called "Pre," finishing off the podium was a bitter disappointment. Check that. The guy could have cared less about being on the podium. If he didn't leave Germany with the gold medal, the trip to Europe, in his mind, would have been a horrific waste of time.

Kenny Moore recalls running into Pre in the bowels of the Olympic Stadium after Moore had finished fourth in the marathon. "I was struggling with how I should feel about the experience," Moore recalls. "I had had a great race, but I hadn't medaled."

Pre put his hands on Moore's shoulders and told him that he was the fourth best marathoner on the planet and that he should be incredibly proud of his achievement. Moore then asked Pre how his 5000-meter event had turned out: "I took *fourth*," he said, barely spitting out the number. "Fourth is awful."

The message was clear: While fourth place was just fine for the Kenny Moore's of the world, fourth is certainly not up to the standards or expectations of one Steve Roland Prefontaine. At one time, Pre held every American record for the seven distances ranging from 2000 through 10,000 meters. He was the James Dean of American running with his long hair, mustache and always-race-from-the-front attitude.

Rod Dixon also had long hair and a mustache, but his style of racing differed from Pre. "I raced to win," admits Dixon. "I didn't want to prove that I could push the pace harder or longer than anyone else. I wanted to be the first person across the line."

Four years earlier, in 1968, Dixon was sitting on a river bank near his home in Nelson, New Zealand, listening to the finals of the Olympic 1500 meters from Mexico on his transistor radio. "The signal was coming in and out and the static made it hard to hear," he recalls.

In the finals, the two leading men were running legends Kip Keino of Kenya and America's Jim Ryun. "I was glued to the radio listening to the finals and hoping that one day I would be the one running the 1500 at the Olympics. That was my dream."

How about this for a dream come true? Four years later, Dixon lined up for the first round of the 1500 in Munich. "On my left was Kip Keino," he says, "and on my right was Jim Ryun." Not only did he run the 1500, he took home the bronze.

A few weeks after Munich, he was in London at a post-Olympic track meet at the Crystal Palace and both Dixon and Pre were entered in the 2-miler.

"Pre was coming down from 5000 and I was stepping up from the 1500," says Dixon. "I sat on him and outkicked him at the end. He broke the American record, and I broke the Commonwealth record, but Pre was upset at me for not sharing the pace. I walked up to him after the race to shake his hand and he called me a f***ing Kiwi and stormed off."

In 1973 Dixon was in Milan, Italy, to race the summer circuit with his good mate, fellow Kiwi and the world record-holder in the mile John Walker.

"Pre was traveling with Ralph Mann, and we ran into the two of them at a bar before one of the races," Dixon recalls. "Mann asked us if we knew Pre, and we all ended up drinking beer for most of the evening. There were probably 13 or 14 empty quart bottles on the table when we called it a night. We set up a time with Pre to run two hours the next day."

During that run, Walker and Dixon took turns making Pre's life miserable. Walker would surge, Pre would respond, Dixon would relax. Then Dixon would attack, Pre would answer and Walker would catch a breather. Their game of two-on-one lasted for the better part of the run; but by the time they were finished sweating in the mid-morning sun, the three were friends for life.

"We had spent two hours dripping sweat, and it was a great run," recalls Dixon. "We told him afterwards that if he ever wanted to be a Kiwi, he had passed the test."

Even though Pre never beat Dixon indoors or out, there was a sense that Pre was going to be unbeatable by 1976 and the Montreal Games.

"I remember watching one of his workouts," Dixon says. "He did two one-mile repeats with 10 minutes of recovery between them. Mile one was 4:01 and mile two was 3:58. He was just so tenacious."

Pre and Dixon would race mainly the 1500, 2-miler or the 3000.

"Pre was constantly working on his speed because he knew that in 1976 he wouldn't be able to run away from the other guys at 5000 meters," says Dixon. "In 1960, a Kiwi named Maury Herbert took off with three laps to go and ended up winning the gold medal in the 5000. Pre and I talked about that race. He figured that if he pushed the pace with three laps to go, he could make it really tough for the other guys. Then he could sit in and wait until 600 to go to make a final move."

There was a sense of arrogance that came with Steve Prefontaine. But, according to Dixon, if you felt you were one of the best in the world, how could you help but not feel a little above the other guys.

"People said that Pre was arrogant," says Dixon. "But remember, I lived with John Walker, who was pretty arrogant himself. Pre knew that if he had doubt, that the other guys in the field had it as well. Pre didn't really have that killer instinct, but he knew what it took to be the best. He was never afraid of the pain. We played hard . . . but we trained harder."

Steve Prefontaine died in a tragic car accident in on May 30, 1975, at the age of 24. Rod Dixon went on to have an amazing career and to win the New York City Marathon in 1983 with a 2:08:59. He came from behind to catch England's Geoff Smith in the last quarter-mile in one of the greatest marathon moments in history.

As honored as he had been as an Olympic medalist, the win in New York City was the defining moment of his career and changed his life forever. But when he is with the high school kids that he works with around the country through his Kid's Marathon Program, kids want to talk to him not because of what he did in New York but because of the young man from Coos Bay, Oregon, who they have read so much about – the guy Rod Dixon used to train and race with.

"They want to shake the hand of the guy who raced with Steve Prefontaine," he admits. "He was special. Nearly four decades after his death, Pre's legacy lives on."

A TAINTED MEMORY

The date was October 2, 1968, just days before the summer Olympics would be starting in Mexico City. Young John Howard was a cyclist on the U.S. team that was training in Mexico at the time to try and acclimatize to the high altitude they would be facing in a few weeks. "I was fresh out of the Ozark Mountains, so this was a pretty special time in my life," recalls Howard.

As he and his teammates watched on the news each day, it was obvious that the college students in the country did not appreciate their nation spending so much money to bring the Olympics to Mexico when people were starving in the street. It was an era of college protests around the world, and Mexico was certainly not immune. There were constant demonstrations, and the President at the time, Gustavo Diaz Ordaz, was determined to stop the marches before the world's media arrived for the Games. He ordered the army to occupy the largest university in the country, The University of Mexico, to try to slow down the protestors.

The students had been on strike for nine weeks, and the demonstrations had gotten progressively larger. Over 15,000 students took to the streets that October day and marched through the city. That evening, over 5,000 gathered at the Plaza de las Tres Culturas in Tlatelolco for another rally.

What Howard and his teammates saw in the paper the next day made him ill. The police, who had brought in armored cars and tanks, opened fire on the unarmed crowd and hundreds of protesters were killed and injured. The estimates of the death toll in the massacre ranged from 200 to 400. The Mexican government did their best to remove the bodies from the streets and sidewalks, arrest anyone who was still breathing and cover up their crime before the world's media arrived to celebrate the "spirit" of the Olympics.

"It's hard to celebrate the purity of sport when there is blood running in the gutters," says Howard. "I'm pretty sure that's not what the Olympic founders had in mind. The regime buried the story. There was a huge cover-up."

But Howard was in Mexico City to ride his bike and to represent his country. So on race day, he was in the American pit area pumping up his tires when he heard an explosion. Startled, he turned quickly and came face to face with a young protester who had put a gun into his mouth and pulled the trigger. It is a visual that Howard has had to live with for over 40 years. "Our eyes met right after he shot himself," recalls Howard. "And it's something you don't ever forget. Why he picked our pit area I'll never know. I started the biggest race of my life with his blood splattered on my lily-white USA cycling jersey."

Needless to say, Howard was so shaken up he had a difficult time focusing on the race and finished out of the medals. His career since that fateful day is legendary. At one time he was the fastest man on a bicycle, going over 150 miles per hour on the Bonneville Salt Flats wearing full leathers and cycling in the draft behind a race car. He was named the cyclist of the 1970s, won a gold medal in the Pan American Games, was on three Olympic teams, won the 1981 Ironman Triathlon and to this day, even in his 60s is one of the toughest guys in the peloton any time he goes out on a training ride.

He has a treasure chest full of amazing accomplishments and memories. But no matter how far or how fast he rides his bike, he has one memory that he can never escape. Even after over 40 years it is too fresh, too vivid and too disturbing to ever go away.

THE HOLY GRAIL

You can tell it still hurts. When you ask Davis Phinney to think back to July 29, 1984, America's winningest cyclist of all time – the guy nicknamed the Cash Register because of his amazing array of sprint finish wins – the color washes out of his face, and he just goes blank.

To understand the day, to understand why that memory is still so raw, it is important to know a little bit about Phinney and his adversary, Alexi Grewal. As Phinney himself will tell you, once he got a taste of winning, he was ravenous. Winning wasn't just something he did after a lead-out from his buddy and long-time teammate Ron Kiefel pretty much every weekend of the year; it was who he was.

Phinney was a winner, and anything less was unacceptable. He was one of the first cyclists to train year-round to refine his craft. On race day, while the rest of the guys were getting settled waiting for the criterium in South Dakota or Colorado or Montana to get going, he was busy cruising the course in the opposite direction. When he got to the point where he came up close and personal to the entire frothing-at-the-mouth peloton, he simply spun his bike around and backed into the front row. His message was simple: Boys, the winner has arrived. Make room for Daddy. I hope you enjoy second, third, 20th, or whatever the hell place you end up in.

He had learned his lessons the hard way. As a youngster, Phinney and his dad, who didn't quite know what to make of his son's growing fascination for riding around in tight fitting black shorts, had driven in the family's Volkswagen van from Colorado to Kentucky for the Junior National Championships. They were camped next to the LeMond family, which included young Greg and grandma and grandpa among others.

"Greg was so irrepressible back then," Phinney recalls. "He was always a bright light radiating energy."

LeMond was also soon to become the greatest cycling talent America had seen – up until another guy named Lance Armstrong arrived a decade later.

Phinney started the road race in Kentucky that day and flatted in the first 100 meters. "I was riding the same set of tires I'd been riding on all year long," he says. "My dad was down the road, and he saw the peloton with about 220 cyclists in it and figured I was somewhere in the pack. Then he saw this kid walking way in the distance. He thought, 'That poor kid . . . he's so far back,' until he realized that that poor kid was me. After driving all the way across the country and after only 100 meters, I was out of the race. I learned early on that I needed to do anything and everything to be great. I didn't have the raw talent of LeMond or Armstrong. I had to be better trained and better prepared than the other guys."

One time the national team was racing in Mexico. Phinney, of course, had packed meticulously and gone over his check list over and over again. LeMond? He just grabbed a duffle bag and threw everything in it – except his bike shoes.

Yep. They were in Mexico during the era where your cleats were hammered into the bottom of the shoes and your shoes really weren't meant to fit anyone else. LeMond borrowed Phinney's spare pair, shoved toilet paper into the toe box so that they could sort of fit, and then went off the front and killed everyone.

"That was Greg," says Phinney. "He could drink out of the tap in Mexico and never get sick. Me? All I had to do was look at some lettuce and I had stomach issues."

Alexi Grewal was the wild one, the guy who grew up riding a horse in Wyoming and loved the feeling of freedom and the exhilaration he got from that. When the family moved to Aspen, Colorado, the only thing that changed was his mode of transportation. Instead of cruising around on Mr. Ed, Grewal started riding and loving his bike. Independence was his. All he needed to do was be willing to turn the pedals. When he rode up, ironically enough, Independence Pass in under two hours, it was obvious he could compete with the best.

Being the rebel, it was only a matter of time until Grewal butted heads with the Polish-born coach of the United States team, the legendary Eddie Borysewicz, known to everyone as Eddie B.

Grewal won the 1984 Olympic Trials, so he was guaranteed a spot on the four-person team that would race on the 12-lap, 118.2-mile course with 300,000 screaming spectators lining the streets of Mission Viejo, California, on July 29, 1984, at the Summer Olympics. Ron Kiefel, Thurlow Rogers and Phinney were the other three. Rogers and Kiefel were under orders to work for Phinney during the race. Grewal, who hadn't seen nor heard from Eddie B. in three or four months, was on his own program.

"I couldn't stand Eddie and Eddie couldn't stand me," Grewal insists.

For the six days leading into the road race, Grewal had been living in a home three miles from the course and riding the circuit a number of times every single day. He knew every climb, every downhill, every turn, by heart.

"I ran into Eddie 20 minutes before the start of the race," Grewal recalls. "He told me we would be working for Phinney that day. I knew I had been riding good, and I told my personal coach that there was no way I could lose."

To make sure of that, he had a buddy stationed on the course so that he had his own personal feed zone for race day. "Yeah, I knew it was totally illegal," he laughs, "but that's life!"

His thought was that he could hit the U.S. team's feed zone and, if he missed it, he had his own to fall back on. "Hey, it would be easier for them to feed three rather than four," says Grewal. "I had it coming and going!"

He knew that his chief rivals that day were Phinney, his teammate, and Steve Bauer of Canada. Early on, Grewal attempted to take a little something out of everyone's legs. "I would do little surges and Bauer would go," he says. "I drew Bauer out and had him turn on that locomotive and really pick up the pace."

Phinney had watched on a small black and white television as his wife-to-be, Connie Carpenter, won the gold medal in a sprint finish with Rebecca Twigg that morning. The stage was set for the couple to both win gold medals that day.

"I was so prepared and so focused," Phinney continues. "I had the best day physically that I ever had on a bike. I felt too good."

Too good? That's right. Phinney chased down every attack and reeled it in. "I was so strong, I led half the darn race," he exclaims.

Which is exactly what Grewal wanted him to do. While Phinney was going hard and having problems getting fuel from the untrained helpers at the feed zone, Grewal was loading up at the USA's feed zone and at his own. His bike jersey pockets were jammed with food.

"I asked Alexi if I could have something to eat late in the race because there was stuff coming out of his pockets," recalls Phinney. "He looked straight ahead and said no. I knew he was on his own mission."

Phinney had dug himself a hole, and Grewal was more than happy to watch Phinney crawl into it and then cover him up.

"I'm into personal responsibility," says Phinney. "I don't blame Alexi. My job was to win the race, and I made too many mistakes. I wasted too much energy."

"It was the best day I ever saw Davis have," admits Grewal." His problem was that he didn't ration himself. My job was to stretch him and make him go too hard too often."

With about 18 miles to go, Grewal took off. The ABC cameramen were sitting on motorcycles right in front of Thurlow Rogers and Phinney when the break happened.

"Thurlow asked me what we should do," recalls Phinney. "I told him that we couldn't chase down our own teammate on national television. We had to block and keep the others from chasing Alexi down."

Grewal had a minute on the field. Little did Phinney and Rogers know that the ABC cameras were not even rolling at the time. "If I had known that, I would have chased his ass down," insists Phinney.

At that point, there was about one lap left, and Phinney was desperate for food and water. "I was dying," he admits.

Just as Phinney was grabbing a bag from the last feed zone, Steve Bauer attacked. "I had to throw down my bag and try and chase him," he says. "Steve was 20 meters ahead when I exploded. It was over. I can still see myself grabbing that bag and watching Steve sprint up the road. My legs froze and the two Norwegians went by me. They didn't even need to accelerate."

What people forget is that back in 1984 there were pro and amateur cyclists. Pros raced in Europe and competed in events like the Tour de France for money. That's where Greg LeMond made his name. Pros could not compete in the Olympics.

For Davis Phinney and Alexi Grewal , the Olympics was everything. "The gold medal was the Holy Grail," says Grewal. "It's like being a drug addict, and the gold medal is the biggest dose you are ever going to get."

Grewal nosed out a hard-charging Bauer for the Holy Grail and, 25 years later, it is something he thinks about a lot. "At the time I had no idea how much it meant," he says. "It's interesting. When I crossed the finish line I felt like I went from the physical to the non-physical and back again. It was a trippy experience. Winning the gold medal was special. I have never been so honored in my life."

For Phinney, taking fifth place did little to console him. "It was the most bitter loss of my life," he insists. "It took me years to get over it. When you want something that bad . . ."

Phinney's voice tails off to a whisper. His career did take off after the Olympics, and he was one of the early members of Team 7-Eleven. He won 300 national and international races in his career, including a stage of the Tour de France, an Olympic bronze in the team time trial, four national championships, a U.S. Pro title in 1991 and a gold medal at the Pan American Games. Connie Carpenter, his wife, retired after winning her gold medal and their son, Taylor, was an Olympian in 2008 cycling on the track in Beijing.

Since 2000, Phinney has been battling Parkinson's Disease and launched the Davis Phinney Foundation to help find a cure.

Grewal's career tapered off over the next 10 years with no achievement ever coming close to his gold medal ride through Mission Viejo in 1984. After retiring, Grewal knew he would have a hard time finding something to replace cycling in his life.

"It's hard to find anything as exciting and meaningful as cycling was for me," he says. "You make your own schedule, you make good money, and you have the freedom to just close your eyes and pedal. What could be better than that?"

OUTKICKED BY A 14-YEAR-OLD

The scene is the 1981 Ironman triathlon in Hawaii. Yours truly is the bearded lunatic, and the blue item that I am wearing like a backpack is actually a precursor to the iPod called Bone Phones. The idea was fairly simple. The straps went under the arms and the stereo and speakers wrapped around the neck. The sound, when it actually worked, was supposed to vibrate off your bones to give the user true stereo.

More often than not, it was static in stereo. But for killing time during a day in the lava fields, Bone Phones were certainly better than nothing.

The other guy is 14-year-old Rob Englehardt, now in his late 40s and a producer of documentary films in Los Angeles. Back in 1981, he was a football star who, through no fault of his own, ended up at the starting line of the fourth-ever Ironman. He happened to realize later that he liked football a heck of a lot more than running around in a Speedo. During college, he played football at Stanford and loved every minute.

"It was a lot more fun to knock the crap out of someone than to sit on a bike seat for seven hours," he admitted later during an interview.

We met while he was traveling to Hawaii with a group of Navy SEALS who his dad worked on as a chiropractor. It was over ice cream a few months earlier when one of the SEALS suggested that Englehardt join them and become the youngest person to finish Ironman.

"I hadn't swum more than 25 feet in my life," laughs Englehardt. "The next thing you know I'm swimming, running and doing 30-mile rides on the weekends."

139

On Ironday, I swam nine minutes faster and rode six minutes faster than Englehardt. That still didn't stop him from running me down 10 miles into the marathon.

"That bike ride crunched me," says Englehardt. "It really picked me up to catch Bob Babbitt during the run. I thought he would be way up there."

Not quite. As we headed into town, we were side-by side. I figured we would finish together. The reality? If I picked up the pace, I'd have the satisfaction of outkicking a 14-year-old. But if he made the first move? I'd have the distinction of getting beaten by a 14-year-old.

No matter how you sliced it, there really wasn't much upside for the bearded one.

"When I saw the finish line, I just started sprinting," recalls Englehardt. "I assumed Babbitt would be with me the whole way."

At least part of the way. In one photo taken that day, we are shown definitely together. Another photo – which I have since destroyed – was taken about 25 yards later, and by then I am in a totally different ZIP code, barely visible over Englehardt's left shoulder.

Our final times? Rob Englehardt, 13:54:53 and Bob Babbitt, 13:54:54.

Since the age limit is now 18, I am part of a very small club. I have the distinct honor of being one of the few people to actually get outkicked by a 14-year-old at the Ironman.

How sweet is that?

ONE AND DONE

Linda Sweeney remembers reading an article on 1979 Ironman champion Tom Warren in *Sports Illustrated*. Living in Tucson, Arizona, at the time and training with her boyfriend and stud runner Thom Hunt (he would go on to set the American record for 10,000 meters on the road with a 28:12 in 1981), Sweeney was intrigued. She was a competitive swimmer and loved running. "The distances of the Ironman sounded stupid and ridiculous," she remembers thinking. "But a seed was planted."

She made the decision to do the 1981 Ironman, sent in her entry fee and started training. "I knew I was really fit," says Sweeny, who was 22 at the time, "but I had no expectations. It was more like, 'Yeah, I think I'll do that.' When you're young you have this tendency to make decisions and just go for it. You ignore things like the fact that you don't ride or own a bike."

Hunt and Sweeney basically made up the training as they went along. "I tried to do two things every day," she recalls. "I would always run, and then I would rotate days swimming or cycling. There really was no theory behind my training."

Hunt bought her a $300 Centurion, and they flew to Hawaii two days before the big race.

Out of the water in 1:02, she was surprised by what she encountered on the Queen K Highway. "I remember reading that the net elevation gain was zero," she says, laughing. "So I figured the bike course was flat."

Not quite.

"In retrospect it was better for me not to know how tough it was," she says. "Denial is a very powerful thing."

Being new to cycling, she wasn't comfortable shifting gears. "I only used two gears all day," she admits. "One for climbing and one for descending."

She had a side-view mirror on the bike along with reflectors, cages on her pedals so she could pedal 112 miles in her running shoes and, of course, a basket on the front.

A basket? "After the swim I put my towel in there," she says. "Plus my cassette player and cassettes." She rocked out to The Who, Blondie and The Tubes. "My favorite song was 'White Punks on Dope,'" she continues.

Hunt rented a moped and followed Sweeney on the bike and run, snapping photos along the way. After her 6:53 bike ride, she ran a 4:04 marathon to win the fourth-ever Ironman World Championship.

While she enjoyed winning and watching herself on ABC's *Wide World of Sports* a few months later, she never did another Ironman. She was injured going into the 1982 race and then moved full-time into running. "I never liked to race," she admits. "I love to train, but the racing part always seemed inconvenient to me."

She recently took the 5-foot-tall Ironman trophy that she won back in 1981 and cleaned off 30 years of dust. It's now proudly on display next to her fireplace. She is one of the few champions who raced the Ironman once, won and never came back. Today she is executive director of the Corporate Directors Forum in La Jolla, California.

On occasion the Ironman will come up at parties, and someone will mention that Sweeney actually won the most important event in the sport.

"One time I was at a space shuttle launch in Florida with a friend who was a shuttle pilot," she says. "He's telling everyone that I won the Ironman. These were people who had been on the Space Station and were actual rocket scientists, and they were intrigued by the fact that I had won this Ironman race. There is so much awe and respect for the Ironman. That part always amazes me."

MEANT TO BE

The date was October 14, 1989. A bobblehead and a poster commemorating the occasion sit on my bookcase. The figure on the left is six-time Ironman world champion and the first inductee into the Ironman Hall of Fame, Dave Scott. The figure on the right is Mark Allen, who had dominated throughout the world during the 1980s but had always come up empty in Kona.

In the fall of 1982 during his first Ironman attempt, Allen rode up next to the 1980 champion Dave Scott on their way to Hawi and said something along the lines of, "Hey, what if we go for a run after this?"

Scott, who would soon be known as "The Man," was not amused. He slapped his bike into a bigger gear and took off. When Allen tried to do the same, his derailleur malfunctioned, and the next thing he knew he was out of the race while Scott cruised to his second title.

It went on like that for almost a decade. Dave Scott won in 1983 and Allen took third. In 1984, Allen built a huge lead during the bike ride and high-fived his way down Alii Drive, figuring the race was in the bag. But midway through the marathon, Allen was out of gas and walking while Scott was flying. That was win number four for Scott while Allen hungered for just one.

In 1986 Allen took second to Scott, and in 1987 Allen built up a five-minute lead early in the marathon before Scott ran him down – again.

Allen was unbeatable the rest of the year in the rest of the world. But when he came to Kona, Hawaii, he was entering Dave Scott's turf – and both of them knew it.

In 1988, Scott pulled out before the race with a knee injury. It was finally Mark Allen's golden opportunity. No Scott, no problem, right?

Wrong. Allen ended up flatting twice and ended up fifth.

It's said that good things come to those who wait. It's also said that some things are just meant to be. When the Boston Red Sox finally won the World Series in 2004 after enduring the Curse of the Bambino for 86 years, the fact that they came back from being down three games to zero to the hated New York Yankees before moving on to the World Series suggests it was meant to be. It wouldn't have meant as much to the Red Sox to finally win the title if they hadn't taken down the Yankees along the way.

Mark Allen can relate. On October 14, 1989, Allen and Scott had a race for the ages. It was Allen's seventh time to Kona, and he did everything right. He stayed on Scott's feet during the swim, shadowed him throughout the bike and was glued to his side during the marathon as the two made a shamble of the field and took more than 18 minutes off Scott's course record.

Allen ran 2:40:04 and Scott ran 2:41:03 that day. They were together until less than two miles were left in the race. Allen made a move on the last uphill, and Scott fought to stay with him.

When Allen came across the line, tears were streaming down both cheeks. He had tried so hard for so long and had finally beaten The Man – fittingly, on the best day Scott ever had on the Kona coast.

That race, Iron War, is frozen forever in my mind's eye.

For Mark Allen it was a day – and a moment – that was just meant to be.

DAVE SCOTT'S SIGNATURE STYLE

It was hard to miss. The jagged, red scar started under the hairline on the right side of his face and traversed his forehead before plunging south in front of the right ear and coming to an abrupt halt just below the chin.

The owner of this distinctive mark, "Jim," was next in line to meet Dave Scott. I was standing behind the six-time Ironman world champion as he signed autographs and chatted with his fans prior to his comeback race, the 1994 Ironman World Championship.

Scott was 40, but he certainly didn't look it. From the long lines, it was obvious that "The Man" had lost little in the way of popularity even though it had been seven years since his last Ironman victory and five since Iron War, the 1989 showdown that he had lost to his nemesis, Mark Allen.

Scott does not simply sign autographs. Nope. He likes to know the people he is signing for. He asks about you, your family, your ancestors, your dog, your dog's ancestors and about that great sandcastle you built back in the third grade.

For people working the booths, he could be maddening. At the end of the day, everyone else has packed up and headed off to dinner while the line to meet Scott still stretched from here to Newark and back. "Dave, my clothes are going out of style," they'd say through clenched teeth. "Dave, I need to get home before my 6-year-old graduates from college."

Scott couldn't care less. He takes the right amount of time with each and every person. They've waited in line to meet Dave Scott, not just to get a scribbled autograph from someone who is fulfilling an obligation and not very happy to be there. Scott is happy to be there and is as anxious to meet you as you are to meet him.

Sound unique? It is. Dave's interaction with the scarred man back in 1994 exemplifies the champion's character.

Jim put a poster in front of Scott, who looked up, smiled, shook hands with his new best friend and started the interrogation:

"Jim, are you racing this year?" says Scott, felt-tip marker at the ready.

"No, not this time," replies Jim.

Scott: "Is someone in your family racing? Your wife? Your brother? Your dad or mom?"

Jim: "No, Dave. No one I know is racing."

Scott: "Are you thinking about doing the Ironman someday?"

Jim: "I'm not really sure, Dave."

Scott was stumped. Jim wasn't racing, no one in his family was racing, and he wasn't here doing reconnaissance.

Scott: "So, what brings you to Kona, Jim?"

Jim: "I'm sure you don't remember, but I was in a car accident four years ago, and a friend of mine asked you to call me. You called me three times while I was in the hospital to see how I was doing. You have no idea what that meant to me. I vowed right then that if you ever raced again in Hawaii, I would be here. I'm here in Kona for one reason: to watch you race."

That year, at the age of 40, Dave Scott ended up finishing second to Greg Welch, adding to his legend. In his career in Kona, he won six times, took second three times and fifth once.

His first Ironman title came in 1980, when he was 26. He broke the course record by nearly two hours that day and proceeded to become the first to go under 11, 10 and 9 hours, and to dip under 8:30. When he lost to Mark Allen in 1989, he went 8:10:13, taking 18 minutes off of his own course record, and running the marathon in 2:41:03. Dave Scott was constantly pushing the Ironman envelope.

Jim was certainly not alone. I admit it. I always loved the Ironman, but when a certain somebody was on the starting line, the buzz factor went through the roof.

Why? Simple. We knew we'd get to watch Dave Scott race.

PLAYING CATCH ON THE QUEEN K

When the 20th anniversary of *Competitor* magazine approached in 2007, I spent a fair number of evenings looking through our amazing archive of images. Every time I look at this one particular image, it makes me laugh.

Scott Tinley ("ST") is on his way to winning his second-ever Ironman Triathlon in 1985, wearing his own line of funky clothing and devoid of his trademark mustache. Back then there were no other Ironman events in the states. This was long before Lake Placid, Panama City, Coeur d'Alene, Madison and Scottsdale. Yeah, there were a few Ironman events around the world, but Kona, then and now, was still the whole enchilada.

The sport was growing, but still incredibly small. Nowadays the leader of the Ford Ironman World Championship is always surrounded on all sides by television cameras, helicopters, officials, sponsors, spotters and media vehicles. Back then? It was ST, our convertible, me, my partner Lois Schwartz – the world's greatest sports photographer – and the driver. No one else was in the same ZIP code.

Tinley had come off the bike a few minutes behind Chris Hinshaw but caught him early in the marathon to take the lead. Hinshaw would finish over 25 minutes back, and third place was another 10 minutes behind him.

Quite frankly, while Tinley was on his way to his second and final Ironman World Championship, the guy was bored to tears. We chatted about the race and how good he felt. The next thing I knew, the two of us were playing catch with a mini football that I happened to have in my pack.

It's the Ironman World Championship. Scott Tinley is about to win his second-ever title. And we're playing catch.

When you think of it, in the scope of today's perception of the event, it's pretty bizarre. It was like he wasn't in the middle of a major championship and there were no other people in the event. We were oblivious, simply playing catch and chatting about whatever came into our minds:

Me: "You doing dinner anywhere special tonight?"

ST: "Not sure. What are you guys doing?"

Quite frankly, at the time it made perfect sense. When the San Diego Track Club introduced the sport of triathlon back in the 1970s, people like Tinley and others like him hopped on board to do something that was a little different. It was really all about getting away from running the roads for a day or two. How much running could you really do without breaking down or having your brain turn to mush?

So run, bike and swim was all about creating variety and options, not creating a new fitness craze or an Olympic sport. Tinley was going to become a paramedic. Dave Scott was a swim coach. Mark Allen was a lifeguard. Scott Molina was flipping burgers at a K-Mart in Pittsburgh, California.

None of us realized that this escape from the grind of running was going to become a vibrant, sexy, dynamic sport all its own with prize money races in every state and in every nation. Hey, if people were going to RACE this new sport, they sure needed people to COVER it, right?

Neither Tinley nor I realized that we would one day make our livings doing exactly what we loved most. He would race, and I would write. Both of us would pinch ourselves every day hoping that no one would ever pull the plug on our fun and make us get real jobs.

Playing catch on the Queen K Highway would probably get the leader of the Ford Ironman World Championship disqualified nowadays for getting outside aid.

Back then?

It was just two guys loving their new sport and sharing a pretty special moment in time.

WHY NOT DROP OUT?

"I will run 2:45 in the marathon."

Pauli Kiuru of Finland was sitting at the pre-Ironman press conference in 1994 talking about what might happen two days later out on the lava fields. Greg Welch and Kiuru, who finished second in 1993, were considered the ones to watch.

A man who never leaves home without his heart rate monitor firmly in place, the book on Kiuru was that he would be right there all day long. Welch might be the more talented of the two in the run but, if he faltered, if the heat zapped him, Kiuru could — and should — win the whole enchilada. Especially if he got off the bike and ran a 2:45 marathon as he had just predicted.

Welch has had a series of tough moments during the Ironman, especially in the marathon. He'd be running great one minute and walking the next. That was his pattern. But no one expected that Kiuru, Mr. Consistent, would be the one to have a tough day.

I guess that's why they race the race. Résumés are nice, but past performances mean absolutely nothing in a game like the Ironman. If you are having a bad day in the lava fields, you can't fake it like you can in a shorter race.

Pauli Kiuru had a bad day. He finished 207th overall with a time of 10:08:25. "I missed my special needs bag at Hawi and was forced to eat food I normally would not eat," he said afterward. "Last year I felt so good on the bike and in the beginning of the run. I was flying. This year I wasn't flying. I was dying."

So, Pauli, why not drop out?

He wiped the sweat from his eyes and shrugged his shoulders. "I didn't have money for a taxi."

In this day and age, professional endurance athletes realize that a bad race takes as long – or longer – to recover from than a good race. Instead of 8 hours, Kiuru was out there 10 hours. People he had never seen before went by him. Terry Schneider was the 12th pro woman. Kiuru would have been 13th. That's not the kind of performance most professionals like to talk about.

Top marathoners drop out all the time. Among the *professional* men signed up for Hawaii, 49 finished and 13 dropped out. Alec Rukosuev, Rob Barel and Peter Kropko were all pre-race contenders. They never finished. DNF'd (Did Not Finish). Why not? Once they're out of the prize money, why go on? For the t-shirt? For the medal? Not usually.

There is another definition of professional. It is someone who doesn't just bag it when they're having a tough day. It is the athlete who believes in finishing what they start.

Kiuru was 2 minutes behind the leaders at Hawi and 12 minutes back off the bike. "I started out running along Ali'i Drive, but then I had to walk. I walked 10 miles. I tried to run, but I couldn't."

Why not cut your losses? Drop out, get a massage, have dinner. No one would question your motivation. You gave it your best; it wasn't there, so you bagged it. It happens every day.

"I didn't have good reasons to drop out," he insists. "I could still walk." He pauses, bent over, hands on his knees. "If you drop out once, you will do it again."

A habit. Once you opt for the easy way out, when things get tough – and they will – you will turn onto DNF street again. Dropping out gets easier and easier. Triathlon is always a game of conditions: a cold and choppy swim, a windy and hilly bike, a hot run. Conquering the conditions is the name of the game.

It's race day, and you're approaching the red line. You feel you've gone as far as you can. The challenge of triathlon comes when you push beyond your limits, willing yourself past adversity. That's when, as Mark Allen says, you open the door, face your fears head on and keep going.

Pauli Kiuru did not want to finish 207th. He did not want to walk 10 miles of the run. He did not want to be passed by people who should never pass him.

But he did not want to drop out more.

"I don't think it's fair to the race organization," says Kiuru. "I am here to race and do my best. I did my very best today, but I was only able to walk. My mental attitude wasn't winning the race. I was trying to be in the spirit of the event."

CHICKEN SOUP AND A GLOW STICK

Australia's Chris Legh has won 60 races in his career, including Ironman California in 2000 and Ironman Coeur d'Alene in 2004.

People probably remember him best for his dramatic collapse 50 yards from the Ironman World Championship finish line back in 1997. His system had shut down due to dehydration, and he ended up in the hospital having a portion of his large intestine removed.

After losing body parts, most of us would exit stage left and find another sport. Not Chris Legh.

The year was 2001, and he was racing Kona again and suffering issues from the effects of pulmonary edema. "With 60K to go on the bike, I was coughing up blood," recalls Legh. "When I got off the bike, I couldn't run. I walked along Ali'i Drive picking flowers off the trees," he says. "When I tried to run, the coughing would start and my heart rate would skyrocket. So I walked."

When he got to the Queen K Highway, he was able to run. But then he spotted the messenger of doom guarding the Natural Energy Lab. It was the woman who doles out the glow sticks to those Ironman hopefuls who are probably going to finish after dark.

The glow stick passer outer is an equal-opportunity abuser. She doesn't care about your résumé or your double-digit race number. Nope. Her job is to make sure all of the denizens of the dark are glow-stick-enhanced. And in 2001, that included Chris Legh.

As he entered the Energy Lab, his wife, Sarah, was waiting at the top for him to run the approximately four miles in the lab and emerge with about 10K to go.

She waited forever. "Seriously, I think the longest hour of my life was spent waiting for him to come out," says Sarah. "I thought he had dropped dead in there."

Not quite. Her strolling husband had found what all of us glow-stick wearers know to be a fact: The aid stations – aka the "Ironman buffets" – are pretty sweet. "Once I got in there, they handed me chicken soup and bread," Legh says, laughing. "It tasted really good."

He eventually emerged and jogged his way back to town with a fellow Aussie. "He would pass me on the uphills, and I would get him on the downhills," Legh recalls. I figured we'd jog our way in. I just wanted the day over."

During the last mile, his buddy hit the wall. "I basically pushed him on the butt to keep him moving," Legh says.

A hundred yards from the finish, the music and lights jumpstarted Legh's partner, and he took off like he was shot out of a cannon.

So what did Legh do? Even though he was three-and-a-half hours behind the winners and his 5:29:12 marathon was actually about 14 minutes *slower* than his 5:15:27 112-mile bike leg, Legh also sprinted for the line. "I'm thinking, 'Oh crap, what am I doing?'" he recalls.

What he was doing was going for bragging rights. He had been humbled a bit with a glow stick, but there was no way he was losing a sprint, even if it was for 675th place.

Legh and his nemesis ended up with identical times of 11:43:35, with Legh ahead by a nose. "I out-leaned him," says Legh, laughing. "Through the years of racing, you learn that when things turn to crap, you simply have to make the best of it."

BULLY A BULLY

Chris "Macca" McCormack was proud. It was October 2006, and he had just had the race of his Ironman life. Remember, this is an Australian who came to Kona in 2002 ready to dominate after winning pretty much every other race on the planet. He ended up leaving town with not only a DNF (Did Not Finish), but with his tail between his legs after declaring during Ironman week that he would like to win the event six times, like Dave Scott and Mark Allen.

Scott told him it might be a good idea to win once before talking about six.

Early on in the 2002 marathon, he was leading and feeling great. He yelled to his dad that he'd be back in a bit, and then they could celebrate his big win.

Not quite.

"I was already planning my acceptance speech," Macca recalls. "Then it all came crashing down. I had to eat a bit of humble pie."

He had seconds and thirds of that pie in 2003 and 2004. But in 2005, after having a little Coca-Cola out by Hawi, he flew back to town, ran a 2:49 and took sixth, his first Kona top-10 finish.

"That's when I realized I could win," he says.

In 2006, he did everything right and lost. Normann Stadler put together a legendary day, going 4:18 on the bike and following up with a 2:55 marathon. McCormack was only 71 seconds back, but he was proud of the effort. "I had a great race and was beaten by a great champion," says McCormack. "People say that if the race was another mile I might have caught him. If the race was another mile, I don't know if I would have finished," he says, laughing. "I gave it everything I had and lost to a better man on that day."

After the awards ceremony, an interview that Stadler did came back to bite McCormack. Stadler claimed that McCormack was drafting on the bike. The interview was e-mailed to McCormack, who was livid.

Third-place finisher and 2005 champion Faris Al-Sultan was making similar statements. The two Germans were putting up a united front against McCormack.

"The best way to take down a bully is to bully them right back," insists Macca. He decided that in 2007, he would seek out Al-Sultan and Stadler and constantly beat them. "I wouldn't enter until I knew they were racing," he says.

Early in the season, Al-Sultan raced in Dubai. McCormack was waiting. "When I crossed the line, I started my stopwatch," he says. "When Faris finished, I told him I had beaten him by 3:30 and walked away."

Stadler was doing television commentary for the Quelle Challenge Roth race and McCormack was on his way to winning. During the ride, McCormack pulled up next to the car where Stadler was broadcasting. "Hey Normann," yelled McCormack. "In 15 weeks you're going to have to face this in Kona!"

"I wanted those guys to think I was totally nuts," he says.

Totally nuts can pay dividends. Stadler dropped out in 2007 during the bike and Al-Sultan didn't even start. McCormack won his first of two Ironman World Championship titles that year. Was it just physical issues for the Germans, or was the crazy Aussie in their heads? Neither has been higher than 10th in Kona since.

McCormack laughs. He received an e-mail that summer in German. He asked a friend to translate. It was from Al-Sultan's mom asking McCormack to stop picking on her son.

Consider yourself warned. When it comes to getting inside someone's head, Chris McCormack is the hands-down leader of the pack.

AN IRON GENT

Bill Bell was in his late 70s and the picture of health as he strolled onto the Conan O'Brien set a little more than 10 years ago. His walk-on music was Black Sabbath's "Ironman," since he had won the 70–74 age division four times and the 75–79 once on the Big Island of Hawaii. O'Brien was fascinated with the fact that a man nearing 80 was still out there swimming, biking and running ridiculous distances.

"Bill," O'Brien said, "I've got to ask. Why do you do it?"

"Well, there are women at these races that look like all women want to look," Bell said. "And then, when you're done, they always have a beer garden."

"Wait a minute, Bill," O'Brien said, laughing. "So you're doing this triathlon thing for chicks and beer?"

When the crowd erupted in applause and laughter, Bill Bell knew that his work was done – that all that was left was for him to do was to flash his frequent smile and give the audience a huge thumbs-up.

I was with Bell at the Desert Triathlon near Palm Springs, California, in early March 2012 and, even when he was riding or running, he was giving everyone who came near him that same big smile and that same huge thumbs-up.

Back when he was in his 50s, Bell went for a physical and rode a stationary bike for 20 minutes while his heart was monitored. Every fourth beat there was a hiccup of some sort on the EKG machine. "I thought there was a loose connection on the machine," recalls Bell.

The doctor thought otherwise and sent Bell off to see Dr. Ben Rosen, the head of cardiology at USC. "Dr. Rosen told me that he would like me to jog 40 minutes three times a week," says Bell. "I was working all kinds of hours, but I loved the running. I called the doctor and asked if I could do more, if I could start running every day."

His first Ironman came in 1982. Since then he has completed 300 triathlons, 32 Ironman events, 33 half-Ironman events plus 158 marathons and two ultramarathons.

Not long into his racing career, Bell started having issues with race directors. When he began racing, the oldest division was 65 and up. When Bell turned 70, he asked race directors to create a 70–74 division. The answer? No way. There would never be enough 70-year-olds racing to make it worthwhile, they said. But it's tough for a 72-year-old to compete with a 65-year-old. "I'd write letters and make calls," he says.

Bill Bell is nothing if not persistent. The last time he finished in Kona he was 78, but he is proud that four over-80 racers have finished under 17 hours.

Bell and his fellow Iron Gents consistently push the age envelope. "We now have 80–84 and an 85–89 divisions," he says proudly. "And I just finished up getting approval from USA Triathlon for a new age group for us 90–94-year-olds."

Turning 90, the machine doesn't function quite so well. His hearing is going and he has a pacemaker, a bad knee and exercise-induced asthma. He lost his 89-year-old wife, Margie, to lung cancer in February 2013, not long after celebrating their 66th wedding anniversary.

But Bill Bell is still out there racing in his own age division – there are three other 90-plus triathletes on the East Coast – and he feels that triathlon is the reason for his longevity. "I put my brother in the ground before he was 70," says Bell. "Triathlon is special, and it is something I will do forever."

Editor's Note: *After he turned 90 on November 19, 2012, Bill Bell wrote: "Well, another has flown by and I am now 90 years old and to celebrate that great birthday, I had a few of my triathlete and biker buddies accompany me on a ride. Every year we get together and in the past have ridden my age in miles. As I aged, we did the distance in kilometers; this year it is in furlongs . . . God willing, I'll see you all in 2013."*

THANKS FOR BELIEVING

I am not usually a poster guy, but on the wall of my living room I have three large posters hanging side-by-side-by-side. They are from Lance Armstrong's Ride for the Roses weekend in Austin, Texas, and seeing them always made me smile. I go back a lot of years with Lance, back to the early days of his triathlon career. I loved his passion and energy and felt that, at the age of 15 and already swimming and cycling with the legends of triathlon, he would be the next great one after Mark Allen, Dave Scott, Scott Tinley and Scott Molina hung up their Speedos.

But back in the late 1980s, triathlon was not yet an Olympic sport, and Lance was determined to get to the big show, which is why he decided to transition to cycling. After he signed with the Subaru Montgomery Cycling Team in 1990, I was invited to ride along in a chase vehicle with Coach Eddie Borysewicz, aka Eddie B., who had been the architect of the 1984 U.S. Olympic Cycling Team and was now overseeing Subaru Montgomery. Eddie was a former bike racer and coach from Poland who spoke an interesting form of staccato English. As we drove along the quiet roads of Escondido, California, we came up next to Lance. I asked Eddie his opinion. Eddie didn't hesitate or mince words: "Lance have diamond legs . . . next Greg LeMond . . . will win Tour de France."

Eddie was right: Lance was special. After he was diagnosed with testicular cancer on October 2, 1996, we had numerous conversations on my radio show, and very few of them involved racing his bike again. Lance told me how he would spend his days, from waking up in the morning to going to bed at night, reading messages from fellow cyclists wishing him well. "Those messages and those people helped get me through those days," he told me, "and I'll forever be grateful."

"Lance," I asked, "you get through dealing with tumors in your stomach and then find out you have lesions on your brain. How did you handle that?"

"I looked at it as a positive," he insisted. "At that point I felt that it couldn't get any worse, that there had to be a light at the end of the tunnel."

I go back frequently to listen to those conversations, and I always get nostalgic. He was a young man in the prime of life and, rather than being scared to death, he was fearless and had decided to get out of the saddle and attack this insidious disease the same way he attacked the peloton.

When he came back and won his first race as a member of the U.S. Postal Service Team in downtown Austin, I was lucky enough to be there as the announcer as he screamed down Sixth Street and outkicked Chann McRae for the win. Since Austin was Lance's hometown and this happened to be part of Lance's Ride for the Roses weekend, I wondered if Chann had maybe given Lance the sprint. "I grew up here too," McRae said. "No way I'd give him that win. He beat me."

Besides the three autographed posters, I also have two champagne glasses from Lance's 1999 Tour de France victory that Giro Helmets created, a Wheaties box showcasing Lance, *Sports Illustrated* issues with him on the cover, an autographed yellow jersey and a personalized *Competitor* magazine cover from a photo shoot we did in 2002: "For my friend Bob," it says. "Thanks for believing."

I am sad to see what has happened to Lance and to an entire era of cycling. I saw the vindictive side of Lance and had my run-ins with him over the past few years. He told me he was unhappy with me for talking about cycling's drug issues on my show and for interviewing David Walsh (the author of *From Lance to Landis*), drug expert Michael Ashenden, longtime Lance critic Betsy Andreu and three-time Tour de France champion Greg LeMond, among others, on my radio show. When I ran into Lance in 2010 during President Bush's W100 Mountain Bike Ride in Texas, he told me then that Walsh and LeMond were idiots and clowns, Andreu was crazy, and that I should do something to myself that I'm pretty sure is not physically possible.

What do I believe now?

I believe Lance Armstrong overcame testicular cancer.

I believe he created a wonderful organization called The Livestrong Foundation that has done so much for so many.

I believe Lance Armstrong was as talented an athlete as anyone I have ever met.

I believe he not only used performance-enhancing drugs, but that he insisted that those around him use them as well. Tyler Hamilton told me during an interview that while he and the other top cyclists in the Tour de France *wanted* to win, Lance *needed* to win.

Finally, I believe that Lance Armstrong was so corrupted by power that he lost his moral compass and took a tragic wrong turn on his way to seven Tour de France titles and immortality.

CHAPTER 10

Jim MacLaren

GONE BUT
NOT FORGOTTEN

UNBREAKABLE SPIRIT

THE BLAZEMAN

"LIVE LIKE KLAUS"

A MAN WELL LOVED

THE PROMISE

MR. LUCKY

CHAPTER 10 – GONE BUT NOT FORGOTTEN

"I wasn't sure I could do it again. I felt so lifeless at first. People had to lift and carry and push me in wheelchairs. I couldn't really do anything on my own.
But eventually my personality and humor came back. Is it fair that this happened to me again?
Of course not, but life isn't about being fair. It's about moving on."

– Jim MacLaren

UNBREAKABLE SPIRIT

It was a summer day in 2005. I walked to the back of his rented home in La Jolla, California, and Jim MacLaren took me through his typical workout. I imagined that it is quite a bit different from what he did as a 300-pound football player at Yale before he was hit by a New York City bus in 1985, thrown 90 feet in the air and declared dead on arrival.

He recovered from that accident, losing his leg below the knee and basically pulverizing his ribs and internal organs. So what did MacLaren do? He didn't hang out feeling sorry for himself. Instead, he became the Babe Ruth of amputee athletes, running a 3:16 marathon and finishing the Ironman in Hawaii in 10:42. That is, of course, with the level of prosthetic available in the late 1980s – which is like comparing that era's Ford Pinto to a 2005 Ferrari.

Unbelievably, in June 1993, MacLaren was hit again, this time by a truck during a triathlon in Orange County while on the bike. MacLaren was propelled headfirst into a pole and became a quadriplegic. The doctors told him he would never regain much in the way of motor function below the chest and that he would always need a support person with him to help with his daily activities.

The San Diego Triathlon Challenge was created in 1993 as a fundraiser specifically for MacLaren. The goal was to raise $25,000 to buy him a vehicle that he could drive with his hands so that he would have some semblance of independence. That first event raised $48,000. Since then, the Challenged Athletes Foundation (CAF) – established in 1997 – has raised nearly $30 million dollars to help disabled athletes buy the equipment they need to stay in the game of life through sport.

Multiple-time Ironman and XTERRA finisher "One-Arm Willie" Stewart says it best, "Sports make me whole."

MacLaren and I chatted for a moment about his doctor's expectations for him after his second accident. He was told that he would never be able to move again from the chest down.

"I wasn't sure I could do it again," MacLaren admits, thinking back to the dark days after his first accident. "I felt so lifeless at first. People had to lift and carry and push me in wheelchairs. I couldn't really do anything on my own. But eventually my personality and humor came back. Is it fair that this happened to me again? Of course not, but life isn't about being fair. It's about moving on."

With a little bit of help, he got out of his motorized chair and walked – yes, *walked* – along the sidewalk to his exercise room. Once there, MacLaren lowered himself onto a stationary recumbent bike, strapped his feet in and started pedaling – on his own.

Next was another walking trip (again guided by his buddy and personal assistant, Scott) out the front of the house, down the driveway and then back up the driveway.

For MacLaren that day, the effort he put out climbing the driveway was equivalent to struggling up Heartbreak Hill in Boston or Pay 'n Save Hill in Kona nine miles into the Ironman marathon. You could see the effort – and the joy – in his face.

He was breathing hard as he crested the grade. He stopped momentarily and turned around to take in the view of what must seem to him like the summit of Mt. Everest. He looked at me and smiled, politely not mentioning the alligator tears that were streaming down both my cheeks. Then he turned and headed to the backyard where he stood up out of his chair, towering over me at about six-feet, four-inches, and grasped two stretch cords to work his arms. From there, it was a short hike to the pool where he walked on his own in waist-deep water. One lap, two laps, three laps . . . I couldn't believe what I witnessed. You'll never move again from the chest down? Sorry, doc. You don't really know Jim MacLaren, do you?

Here's a guy who is a quadriplegic – who is also missing his lower leg, by the way – who was walking laps in a freezing cold pool while bemoaning the fact that his beloved hockey was on strike . . . like this was no big deal . . . like I just didn't witness a medical miracle.

MacLaren has been challenged more than anyone we will ever know, but he continues to ignore the doctors who tell him that he can't possibly do what I watched him do. Why? Because while MacLaren's body may have been shattered twice, his spirit is unbreakable.

Editor's Note: *Jim MacLaren – at one time the world's fastest amputee triathlete – passed away on August 30, 2010 at the age of 47. His life was short but amazingly impactful. The Challenged Athletes Foundation is Jimmy's legacy. I'm proud to say that, through the athletes we help every day, his impact will live on forever.*

THE BLAZEMAN

It's a photo from the 2000 Ironman California at Camp Pendleton. There is a bicycle belonging to double-above-knee amputee Rudy Garcia-Tolson on a trainer with Rudy's bike legs leaning up against the front wheel. Surrounding the image are the words "What's it going to be today, Blazeman . . . Victory or Death?"

Jon "Blazeman" Blais used the photo as a way to inspire himself to get out of the house and get his training in – and to motivate his students to reach for the stars. A special education teacher at Aseltine School, a private school for behavior issues in San Diego, California, Blais plunged into the sport of triathlon full-bore at the age of 14 on the east coast and never backed off. Being in San Diego gave him every opportunity to run, bike and swim his brains out every day of the year.

He didn't just teach the kids he worked with, he believed in them.

"I was full of piss and vinegar as a kid," he says. "So I guess I was able to relate to kids who were a lot like me."

As a kid one day he decided to dress up as condom man and throw condoms to the crowd. A trip to the principal's office quickly followed. "That was pretty funny," Blais admits.

He was always on the cutting edge, teaching the kids to rock climb and using heart rate training so they could learn about their bodies and empower themselves.

"A lot of these kids try to avoid success," he says. "They stay in their comfort zone and sabotage any chances they might have."

Blais built his following by believing in kids before they believed in themselves. That's what set him apart, what made him special.

In 2003 he competed in 20 triathlons, but in October of that year he didn't feel quite right. When he was working at the school, his body would start twitching a lot. He also found himself swimming off-course. "I'd be at the La Jolla Cove, and I just couldn't swim a straight line," he says.

In January of 2005, he was at a party with some friends and he had trouble holding on to the beer bottle. "I'm a southpaw and hold my beer in my left hand. All of a sudden I had to hold my beer in my right hand," he recalls.

In February he crashed hard on his mountain bike in San Clemente Canyon and ended up with 15 staples in his head. "I never would have had such a stupid accident if I hadn't started to lose control of my hands," he insists.

Being the teacher, he went online and researched the symptoms. "I'd stay up all night researching all the possibilities." He knew that he had ALS (amyotrophic lateral sclerosis), known as Lou Gehrig's

Disease, before the doctors did. "If you have twitching and muscle wasting in more than one limb, you have ALS," he says. "No question about it."

He was diagnosed on May 2, 2005 at the age of 33. Lou Gehrig's last game of his 2,130 game consecutive game streak? May 2, 1939. He had to call his mom at 2 a.m. to tell her that her son had ALS.

When you are diagnosed with ALS it is a death sentence, and you are given two to five years – if you're lucky. There is no treatment and there is no cure.

"About 150,000 people die of ALS every year, 411 a day and 17 per hour," says Blais. "And 350,000 live with it every day. There is no beating ALS. No one has ever done anything but walk away and die."

But Blais is not the type of guy to receive a death sentence and simply disappear. "I knew that I had to raise awareness and funds to fight ALS," he says." I knew I wasn't going to win this battle, but I wanted to go out like a warrior. People who knew me as the Blazeman knew I had to go down fighting."

Anyone who witnessed Blais at the 2005 Ford Ironman World Championship saw the heart of the man. He hadn't been able to train since 2003. He had gained weight and his body was deteriorating rapidly. He rode the bike in August for the NBC crew and then again after he arrived in Kona. That was it. He was racing the toughest race on earth on guts and guts alone.

In his prime he would have swam the 2.4 miles in about 1:05. He was hoping for 1:30. Instead he went 1:50 because he was only able to use one arm, and his body was cramping badly. On the bike he couldn't get out of the saddle, his upper torso felt like a brick and his quads and calves were seizing up with every turn of the pedals. At the turnaround in Hawi, a race official told him that he wasn't going to make the 5:30 p.m. cutoff time.

"I had my special needs bag, so I chucked my banana bread at him," he laughs. "There was no way I was going to miss that cutoff."

The NBC camera crew that had been following him earlier had now disappeared, as his chances of starting the marathon were dwindling. "They took off," he recalls. "They gave up on me and went to film another story."

Fortunately the Blazeman doesn't believe in giving up on the kids he teaches or the dreams he's living. By mile 80 he was back on pace, and the camera crew was there to capture him finishing the bike and starting the marathon with his parents, 20 friends and the entire world there to witness a miracle in the making.

Before the race, Mike Reilly, the voice of the Ironman, had asked Blais what he was going to do at the finish line. A handstand? A cartwheel? A Greg Welch style leap? Blais told Reilly that he didn't know if he was going to finish, that Reilly might have to log-roll his sorry butt across the line.

So when Blais approached the line, that's exactly what he did. In the same way he has dealt with his disease, he proudly took his time, dropped to the ground and log-rolled ever so slowly toward the finish of the race and ever closer to the finish of his life. He took his time and savored every second of the journey.

Jon "Blazeman" Blais died May 27, 2007, at the age of 35. To the very end he was the teacher. He taught us all about a disease that is insidious and totally ignored. And he taught us how to handle adversity. But most of all, he taught us to never, ever give up.

"You can choose to be pissed off, or pissed on," he'd say laughing.

Blazeman, as always, chose the former.

"LIVE LIKE KLAUS"

The moment is frozen forever. The head is tilted back as his eyes search the heavens. With his fists clenched and mouth wide open, the expression is one of pure, unadulterated joy. I squint through the photographer's loop to check out the overhead clock in the photo from the 1986 Ironman. The time is 9:03:42. The place is fourth.

At the time, Klaus Barth was knee deep in applause and adrenaline. His wife Shari and the three kids were sprinting out from behind the barriers to greet him. The Long Beach Wilson High School swim coach had paid his Irondues in full. He collapsed nine miles into the run in 1984 while in ninth place. In 1985, he had finished eighth. When he showed up the following year, he expected to be wearing number eight when he went to the line. That was the rule. Finish first, wear number one the next year. Finish second, wear number two. Not this time, bucko. He was told that they looked upon the 36-year-old's finish from the year before as a fluke, a combination of a lucky day and a weak field.

"I said, 'What the heck, I finished eighth,'" recalls Barth. "They said 'Hey, nobody raced last year. We've set number eight aside for the right guy. That guy unfortunately is not you.'"

His race number come race day was 48. Not bad, but certainly not number eight. He knew he was ready to go after a full summer of 150-mile rides from his home in Long Beach, California, to Solana Beach and back followed immediately by a 10-mile run on the Long Beach Marathon course. His wife Shari and the three kids knew that he was getting ready for the race of his life.

That's why Klaus Barth was so damn happy at the finish. Eighth place? *Forgetaboutit!* Barth proved that eighth was indeed a fluke. He was a year older, 37, and finished fourth. The only guys in front of him? Dave Scott, Mark Allen and Scott Tinley.

Flash forward 13 years to 1999: Klaus Barth was looking to prove people wrong once again. He was hoping to do the Ironman in October at the age of 50. But that dream was trashed when he had both hernia and knee surgery on July 3. It was the old tag team approach: Knock out the hyperactive Barth, have the hernia guy come in and take care of business, then tag off to the knee specialist and have him do his thing.

Then something even more brutal came up. While Barth was in a meeting with his tax accountant one day, he suddenly collapsed to the floor with a grand mal seizure. He was about two minutes away from getting in his car and driving off to swim practice. If he had had the seizure in his car, there would be a good chance that Klaus Barth would have died that day. But he lived and his fight wasn't over.

The cause of the seizure? The doctors eventually found that, besides having the heart of a 20-year-old, he had a brain tumor the size of a gumball called a glioblastoma multiforme, the beast of all tumors. It was a grade 4 out of 4, the worst you can get. The surgery on October 5 took six-and-a-half hours and the tumor was malignant. He finished 33 radiation treatments at an experimental program at UCLA in mid-December and chemotherapy started in early January of 2000.

For the radiation, the doctors strapped a mask to his face and had him lie perfectly still. "They lock you in this room," he says. "First they close an eight-inch thick door behind you. Then they close another 10-inch thick door." He laughs. "It doesn't make you feel very good about what they are pumping into your body."

Whatever they pump in can't be any tougher than the guy they are pumping it into. To get Barth into the very tight UCLA program, Shari sent a copy of the poster that Sparkletts Water had created of Klaus back when he finished fourth in Kona. She mailed it off to the doctors with a note that said: "My husband will make your study look good."

Klaus Barth was accepted the next week.

"I told the doctor that I'm going to be a great subject and a great guinea pig," he recalls. "I'm going to prove everyone wrong."

Barth coached swimming for 18 years, plus soccer and water polo. He knows what hard work, pain and commitment are all about.

One athlete he coached way back when was a high school kid named Tom Gallagher who eventually became a professional triathlete. "Gallagher told me that he was scared of me the first time we met," laughs Barth.

Now he and Gallagher are the best of friends. They have pulled and pushed and prodded each other through a number of workouts and races. In 1987 they finished Ironman side by side.

"We kept looking for the lead helicopter," says Barth. "We were hoping we'd finish in front of the first woman."

Keep hoping, boys. Erin Baker came steaming by the two of them a half mile before the finish. "She was flying," recalls Barth. "There was no way we could go with her."

On the Halloween following Barth's surgery, Gallagher came by the Barth home. He rang the bell like any other trick-or-treater. His costume was one part trick and three parts treat. "The left side of his head was shaved just like mine," Barth recalls. "And he had a scar drawn on the side of his head right where mine is."

Tom Gallagher can't share the pain, but he can sure share the hope.

The fight could be a long one. Shari, the kids, Gallagher, plus Klaus' legion of friends and former students know that all too well.

Barth told Shari more than once, "While I was out on the Ironman bike course, when things got tough, what got me through was thinking about you and the kids."

Times are tough again and the winds are howling. This time, in order to help Klaus Barth get through the hardest ride of his life, he needs all of us to think about him.

My gut tells me that Klaus Barth will prove the experts wrong, that he will come out the other side and live to race again.

You can bet on it.

Editor's Note: *Sadly, Klaus Barth lost his six-year battle with brain cancer (his doctors gave him six months) and passed away on October 22, 2006 at the age of 57. As Klaus wished, the Klaus Barth Foundation was established and is dedicated to providing funding for research and support so that Klaus can still continue to teach and inspire. It is the foundation's desire to continue Klaus's desire to help those battling cancer and support athletes who have physical challenges they must push past in order to meet their competitive goals. For more information, go to www.livelikeklaus.org.*

A MAN WELL LOVED

He asked about the magazine, and we talked about the upcoming Ironman showdown between Mark Allen and Dave Scott. Then, after a little more pre-Friday Night La Jolla Cove Swim chitchat, he said, "Ready to go?"

"Nah," I said. "I'm waiting for my fiancée. Why don't you go on ahead?"

It was September 2, 1989, and as Richard Jernigan walked slowly to the stairway leading to the Cove, I remembered thinking how amazing it was that this guy could do Ironman with legs so bowed he looked like he was auditioning as a John Wayne stand-in. I watched him adjust his goggles, retie his bathing suit and proceed down the stairs to the water's edge. I didn't know it was the last time I'd see him alive.

At 50, Jernigan was a man of many talents. A dentist by trade, he had a way of making you comfortable, of making you actually look forward to coming in for a checkup. He'd sit next to you and fill your mouth with air and water, place his hand and instrument upside some bicuspid or other, then ask you questions about anything and everything . . . politics, cycling, triathlon, mountain biking, scuba diving. You'd be lying there prone in that dentist-chair-from-hell, a bib wrapped around your neck (like the ones from the All You Can Possibly Swallow BBQ Chicken & Ribs stand down the street), gargling and babbling away unintelligibly. And somehow he was always able to decipher what you were saying and respond. You name the topic, and Jernigan could talk about it. Tall and angular, his gray hair and his *Father Knows Best* demeanor made you instantly trust him with your life – not to mention your mouth.

The pictures in his office were all from his underwater photography days. He loved to escape, to go scuba diving or mountain biking whenever possible. If you had a visit scheduled in the spring, you'd see his bicycle in the office. That's because every spring he'd be training for the Davis Double Century bike ride in northern California.

On the day after our last conversation at the Cove, Jernigan went scuba diving with a friend near Bird Rock in La Jolla. He never came back. A heart attack? A diving error? After 30 years as a diver, the latter seems very unlikely. But discovering how he died seems unimportant now. It's how he lived that counts.

The man definitely knew how to live. He jammed more into his 50 years than some of us will do in 80. He was a man who loved life and lived it fully. Among his many accomplishments were completing the Ironman in Hawaii and several Davis Double Century bike rides. He was a tenacious football and rugby player in college – and he had the bad knees to prove it. When the doctors told him it would be tough to keep running with no cartilage in his knees, he didn't miss a beat. "No running? Well, I'll just ride more and scuba."

Jernigan was competitive. One of his best friends was Mark Richert, owner of Chuck's Steak House and founder of Chuck's Triathlon. Richert likes to tell the story about how the two vowed to do the 1982 Ironman together. During the run, however, Richert felt stronger than Jernigan and started to pull away. Jernigan stopped and yelled at him. "We have a deal!" he screamed, and went on to tell Richert that he was expected to live up to the terms of that deal. After all, Jernigan said, a friend is a friend and a pact is a pact. Richert acquiesced, and they continued on together, finally approaching the finish line hand-in-hand. Then Jernigan stepped in front of Richert at the tape and smiled. No one said anything about finishing *exactly* together, did they?

During swim workouts at the pool, Jernigan drove his lane mates crazy, always swimming on their heels, drafting whenever possible. "Richard Jernigan, quit drafting me!" he'd hear on more than one occasion. Jernigan would just shrug his shoulders and smile.

The primary accomplishment of Dr. Richard Jernigan's life was on prominent display the afternoon of his funeral. Both the inside and outside of the church were jammed. It was filled way past capacity with people lining up on the steps and out onto the lawn to pay their last respects. Jernigan was a people person who touched everyone he met in a very positive way. He made you feel good about who you were and what you did. He truly cared about his family, his patients and his friends. And that diverse group of people grew larger each and every year. His funeral served as a celebration of a life well lived by a man well loved.

The Japanese feel that you can't ask for more than to die doing something you love. Richard Jernigan loved to scuba. Our only wish was that he could have hung around for just a few more dives. We'll miss him.

Editor's Note: *On September 4, 1989, the* **Los Angeles Times** *reported, "The body of a scuba diver missing for nearly a day was recovered Sunday afternoon about a mile offshore, lifeguards reported. Dr. Richard Jernigan, 50, a La Jolla dentist, apparently drowned after he became tangled in kelp 60 feet below the surface and ran out of oxygen, lifeguard Lt. Charlie Wright said. Jernigan's partner reported him missing shortly after 6 p.m. Saturday when he failed to resurface after a dive."*

THE PROMISE

While he was in high school, Dustin Brady raced both mountain and road bikes. In 1996 he won the California Junior State Championship on the trails and his division at the Redlands Road Race.

After a number of challenging training days, he could just tell that his body wasn't right. "It's not good when you get back from a ride and can't remember the last 10 miles," he admits. "It's just not safe."

He was diagnosed with type 1 diabetes and would need to monitor his blood sugar for the rest of his life.

His racing career now on the back burner, Brady headed off to college at Cal State Fullerton in Southern California and started working for Shimano. That is when he met Michelle Weiser, the woman who would become his fiancée.

Two years into the relationship, Michelle was diagnosed with stage II breast cancer. The cancer then metastasized into her lungs and it became stage IV, the worst possible scenario.

"We tried to make the best of things," Brady says. "Michelle was all about living life to the fullest. She always said that if there is something you want to do, do it before it's too late."

When Brady went to Kona to support Shimano's Ironman athletes in 2008 and 2009, Michelle came along.

The two of them loved watching the last athletes finishing between 11 p.m. and midnight. "Michelle turned to me and goes, 'You should do this someday,'" he says. "I'm like, 'Yeah, it's on my bucket list.'"

Brady found out before Michelle that she didn't have much time left. "She was having complications," he says. "We went to the hospital, but Michelle wasn't asking the tough questions. I asked a doctor what was going on, and he told me that she had only weeks or months to live. He told me not to tell her, that I had to let Michelle ask the tough questions at her own pace."

When Michelle asked the tough questions – and got the tough answers – her thoughts turned to everyone else. *How was her mom going to handle Michelle's death? How about Dustin?*

"I had gained weight and was pretty unhealthy," Brady says. "Michelle, in her typical sassy way, asked me what I was going to do when she was gone, that I didn't have the life skills to handle things. I blurted out, 'I'll tell you what I'm going to do. I'm going to do an Ironman for you and for me.' She started to tear up, I moved in to hug her and she put her hand up to stop me. Then she put her hand out and goes, 'Do you promise?' I shook her hand and told her it was a promise."

Michelle passed away on July 5, 2010.

Brady's dad made an urn for Michelle's ashes, and Brady had her with him throughout his Kona Ironday on October 8, 2011.

He took the urn out as he crested Palani and Michelle's remains were in Brady's right hand for the last 1.2 miles. "It was overwhelming with all of these people yelling," he says, laughing. "I was like, 'How do they know my name? Oh yeah, it's on my bib!'"

He crossed the line in 16:40:01. All he remembers is Mike Reilly telling him that he was an Ironman and almost tripping.

Two women were in charge of guiding finishers to the post-race area, but Brady broke away from them, took a detour and headed to the beach where his race had begun nearly 17 hours earlier. He then waded into Kailua Bay, opened the urn and scattered Michelle's ashes into the surf.

"We spent the entire day together, and I fulfilled my promise," he says. "Then it was time to say goodbye."

MR. LUCKY

Scott Brown and Chris Fuller fit the profile for Muddy Buddies perfectly. After all, the Land Rover Certified Muddy Buddy is for folks looking for a good time running and cycling with a little bit of pizzazz added to the equation in the form of mud pits, wall climbs and an inflatable or two to get over, around or through.

Brown was 33 at the time of the 2002 Muddy Buddy at MCAS Camp Pendleton north of San Diego, California. He grew up in Kauai, Hawaii and spent his early days surfing and mountain biking. Later he moved to Southern California and added the Muddy Buddy, trail running and a few Hi Tec Adventure races to his athletic résumé.

One day, he was working on his house and felt a little fatigued.

"I told my wife, Marisa, that I was tired, that I needed a nap. She told me that I was getting old and to quit complaining," recalls Brown.

Not long after that, Brown was out surfing in Oceanside with Fuller. He knew this time that something was definitely not right. All of a sudden he was dizzy and his wetsuit felt tight, constricting. He caught a wave to shore.

"I told Marisa what happened, and she told me to go see the doctor," recalls Brown. "I never go to the doctor."

It's nice he made an exception this time. The tests showed that he had an enlarged heart, which for an athlete is normal. But further tests showed that his heart's ejection fraction was 12 percent. What does that mean in English? A normal heart is 50 percent; 35 percent is considered heart failure. Twelve percent? Make sure your papers are in order.

Thirty days later, the doctors installed an AICD (automated implantable cardioverter defibrillator) to help regulate his heart.

Brown still exercised, but his heart was so weak that it was pointless. Plus, whenever his heart rate went over 240, he'd get zapped and wake up on the ground, not really remembering what happened.

"My heart would just take off," recalls Brown. "I would get what is called ventricular tachycardia, which means a rapid heard rate originating from the ventricles. The lower chamber of my heart would start going up to 240 beats per minute and the top chamber couldn't keep up." He could be lying in his bed watching television, and all of a sudden he would feel dizzy. He knew he was about to pass out.

"I would pass out, get shocked and then wake up sweating," says Brown. "Sometimes it would shock me before I passed out, which was really no fun. My life was saved so many times by the AICD."

The doctors were monitoring him all the time. The prognosis? One third of the folks in his position get better, a third stay the same, and the other third get worse.

In February 2004, Brown's condition worsened drastically. His AICD went off at home. On the way to St. Joseph Hospital in Orange County it went off again. While he was at the hospital, it went off eight more times. The next day, while still in the hospital, he had to be cardio converted. You know, like you see on television: the guys and gals with the paddles shocking someone back to life when their heart can't control itself.

"My heart rhythm was not right, and they couldn't get it back to normal," says Brown. "Usually my AICD would go off and get it back to where it needed to be, but this time it didn't work. So they drugged me to get me ready for the paddles. I was out cold, having a dream of some sort. But then I heard someone say 'Are you ready?' It was the doctors about to shock my heart back into rhythm. I thought they were talking to me, so I opened my eyes and said 'ready for what?' The last thing I remember them saying is 'Wait, he's not out . . . give him some more!'"

When his heart rate dropped back to normal, the doctors wanted to transfer him to UCLA; he needed major surgery. The insurance company said that he had to go to San Diego or the transplant would not be covered. Brown's physician, Dr. Kelly Tucker, called the insurance company and told them that if he wasn't transferred to UCLA immediately he would die. Brown was told that he had 24 hours to live and that his organs were shutting down. His options were simple: He needed a new heart or an artificial heart NOW.

There is something called a heart list. Folks who are in the most desperate need are moved to the front of the line. One catch: There still needs to be a heart available for where you are on the list to even matter. The reality is that many have died while waiting for a heart that just never came.

Brown was on the list for all of 30 minutes. Yep, 30 minutes. He was given 24 hours to live and within 30 minutes the doctors were notified of a 17-year-old heart that just became available.

"The coordinator told me she put me on the list, received an immediate response and got the chills," recalls Brown. "She didn't want to tell me until she ran it again just to make sure."

Another point of good karma: The transplant co-director was from Kauai and went to the same high school, Waimea High, that Brown did.

"When he met me and found out that I was from Kauai, he left the room and said, 'I'll have to take care of the Kauai boy.' That made me feel so much better," says Brown.

The next morning, on February 10, Brown was the proud owner of a brand new heart. Five days later, he was out of the hospital. For the first three months he was at home, isolated from the rest of the world and all their colds and infections.

"I was like the Bubbleboy character in Seinfeld," Brown laughs. He saw his doctors every week for a month or so. Then it was every other week and then once a month. Brown laughs again. "They told me to stay out of the dirt."

Fat chance. On August 15, 2004, Brown did just the opposite of staying out of the dirt – he crawled through the mud at the Land Rover Certified Muddy Buddy at Bonelli Park in Los Angeles with his best buddy Chris Fuller. Their name? Team Heart Throb.

Just like in 2002, the two ran arm-and-arm to the finish line, coated with slop from head to toe. It had been a long time since they were able to share a feeling this good. For good measure, Brown actually carried Fuller across the line.

Over the next two years, Brown and Fuller completed two Land Rover Certified Muddy Buddy events in San Jose, California, one in Austin, Texas, and another one in Los Angeles. Plus, the two ran and walked the 2005 edition of The City of Los Angeles Marathon together in March with Brown running as a part of the Saucony 26 program, and, in February, he was honored as their Saucony 26 Man of the Year.

The following summer, the plan was for Brown and Fuller to go to Austin, Texas for the Land Rover Certified Muddy Buddy on Sunday, August 6, 2006. Brown and I were e-mailing back and forth the week before the event when he mentioned that he was having "a little bit of a valve issue." I joked with him that a Ford has a little bit of a valve issue. When it's in your transplanted heart, there is no such thing as a "little" valve issue.

When I returned from Austin on Monday, August 7, there was an e-mail waiting for me from Fuller. Scott Brown, his best friend in the world and the father of two little girls, had passed away over the weekend. The memorial for Scott Brown was held on August 10, which would have been his 38th birthday.

I'll be honest. When my dad passed away in February 2006, at the age of 92, I was able to look at the funeral calmly as a celebration of a life well lived by a man well loved. For Brown's special day, I was a soggy mess. He was too young and had too much left to live for. His girls would have to go on without their amazingly loving dad who told them every single day how much he loved them.

My eyes well up now as I remember scanning the patio that day and seeing one photo of Brown with his hand on his chin, a sly smile on his lips, in his Saucony 26 pose. Then there was another photo from Muddy Buddy with Fuller as they neared the finish. They both had their heads titled back screaming with everything they had to the heavens. Then I thought about all the lives he touched and how many people he inspired in that ridiculously short span of 30 months.

When I first wrote about him, I called Scott Brown "Mr. Lucky." Two and a half years later, I finally realize that the rest of us were the lucky ones.

ABOUT THE AUTHOR

Bob Babbitt is the co-founder of *Competitor* magazine, the co-founder of the Challenged Athletes Foundation, the co-founder and co-host of www.competitorradio.com and the founder of the Muddy Buddy Ride and Run Series. He has authored five books, including the highly acclaimed coffee-table book, *30 Years of the Ironman World Triathlon Championship*, and has hosted television shows for the Outdoor Life Network, Universal Sports and ESPN, among others. He is a recipient of the Paralysis Project of America's Media Awareness Award, a 2012 Inductee into the USA Triathlon Hall of Fame and the 10th inductee into the Ironman Triathlon Hall of Fame. He is currently the editor-at-large for the Competitor Group in San Diego, California.

CREDITS

Photos:

Page 11:	Babbitt Family archives
Page 31, 45 & 59:	Bob Babbitt
Page 47:	Rock 'N' Roll Marathon
Page 81:	Tim Mantoani
Page 97, 111 & 119:	John Segesta
Page 129:	Rich Cruse
Page 131, 155:	Lois Schwartz
Cover photos:	Bob Babbitt, REI Muddy Buddy Series
Cover:	Sabine Groten
Layout:	Claudia Sakyi
Editing:	Sabine Carduck
Copy editing:	Elizabeth Evans, Diana Babb
Typesetting:	Bruno Hilger

STUMBLING TOWARDS THE FINISH LINE

Edited by Kevin Mackinnon

Best of Ironman Columnist
Lee Gruenfeld

NEXT
140.6 MILES

MEYE
& MEYE
SPOR

IRONING OUT IRONMAN
How to Improve the World's Toughest Race

Don't get me wrong: I love Ironman. I wouldn't actually *do* one even if wild crows were pecking out my eyeballs, but I love the sport nonetheless, in much the same way I love, say, crocodile wrestling or *Fear Factor 13: Flirting with Plague*. Which is to say, as a spectator.

But I understand Ironman better than most active non-participating fans, being married to someone afflicted with MESS (Maniacal Endurance Sports Syndrome) and knowing an awful lot of MESS-ed up athletes. Having watched otherwise level-headed people compete in Ironman races around the world, I think I'm eminently qualified to comment on how the sport might be improved, if only those pig-iron-headed know-it-alls at WTC would wake up and smell the VOG.

Herewith a sure-fire set of ideas for ensuring that our favorite sport doesn't go the way of *Gigli*.

1 – The first idea is so absurdly obvious it's hard to fathom that no one's thought of it before:

Make it shorter.

I've thought about it a lot and have come to the conclusion that just about everything that's wrong with Ironman is due to its length. What kind of sense does it make to stage a race that's so long some people can't even finish it? *King Kong* is too long also, and there's nothing that can be done about that now because it's a one-shot deal (okay...one-shot and two remakes). But Ironman can still be edited. Just think of all the benefits.

For one thing, you can get rid of the medical tent, relieving psychic turmoil and buying back some finish line space. Upwards of 13% of all entrants end up in the medical tent, making the finale of the world's most prestigious athletic event look more like an airplane crash investigation than a sporting contest. A cot and a puncture wound in a M*A*S*H tent is why 90,000 people a year compete for a slot?

TThe cost savings alone would be enormous, starting with a lot fewer bananas, water bottles and support personnel. Then there's the reduction in wear and tear among spectators, something race directors have failed to take into consideration from the very beginning. Not to mention equivalent (and sometimes even more severe) wear and tear among the athletes, despite their much-ballyhooed conditioning. Basic corporate economics here, WTC: Why pummel your prime customer base so badly that they can only do business with you once or twice a year? Get the distance down low enough to where an athlete can do thirty, forty races a year and we're talking some serious entry fee revenue here, my friend.

Stumbling Towards the Finish Line

As an added benefit, you foster better relationships with the community. Let's be honest: Not everybody in the deceptively tranquil and purportedly Aloha-soaked Kailua-Kona looks at the annual World Championship the way Kirsti Alley looks at a Mallomar. For one thing, they don't like their main roads getting shut down, a frustration they like to vent by inventing their own sports, like the perennial, week-before-race-day favorite, "Let's see who can drive his 40-ton semi closest to a cyclist without getting a ticket." If the Ironman were entirely confined to a four-block area surrounding the corner of Ali'i and Kuakini Highway and set up so that access to the Blockbuster and Starbucks on Palani remained uninterrupted, why, I'm just guessing that there'd be one or two fewer dirty looks from the guy hawking timeshares from that little booth down by Pancho & Lefty's.

2 – Another one I can't believe no one's thought of yet:

Let's beef up the aid stations.

Mine is not a sophisticated palate and has been described by various snobby acquaintances as roughly akin to a hockey puck when it comes to culinary discrimination. But even I can see that slurping some sucrostic glop out of a foil packet hardly ranks among the world's great gustatory experiences (although I'm told that, when mixed with a goodly dollop of sweat, a certain intriguing piquancy may be achieved).

Try to imagine another event where you pay hundreds of dollars to enter, thousands more to travel there, and all they serve you on the "Big Freakin' Day" is glorified candy bars and sugar water. Out of *disposable bottles*, no less.

It doesn't have to be this way. What would be so hard about a slight upgrade of the menu? And speaking of menus, why does every athlete have to ingest the same stuff as every other athlete? We've got people from Ghana, Liberia, Ecuador and Detroit, and we feed them all the same stuff. What happened to this joyous celebration of multiculturalism the Ironman is supposed to represent?

At a lot of golf courses on the Big Island, there's a telephone mounted on the tee box of the ninth hole that's connected to the restaurant at the club house. There's also a printed menu where the phone book would normally go. You use the phone to place an order before teeing off, then pick up your food as you make the turn to the back nine. Simple, effective, and greatly appreciated by patrons.

So here's what I'm thinking. You know those giant Timex mileage markers? Replace them with menus. Then, a hundred yards later, have a bank of telephones. After athletes pass the menus, they'll have plenty of time to mull over their choices and be ready to call them in when they get to the phones. (Revenue-generating idea: Make them pay phones.) By the time they hit the aid station, their orders will be ready to go.

I keep reading in all these triathlon magazines that there's no reason a healthy diet can't be appealing and delicious as well, so even the kind of limited offerings one expects in the middle of a race should reflect that. What exhausted and numbed-out athlete wouldn't appreciate an appetizer of pâté de foie gras garnished with sprigs of parsley and radish curls, followed half a mile later by a little roast venison with mint sauce accompanied by julienne of potatoes and epinards d'Seville?

Which brings me to another thing: Is there anything in the Ironman rule book about alcohol out on the course? Because it seems to me that washing all of this down with a glass or two of '87 Montrachet would be just the ticket in more ways than I can count. The beneficial effects of red wine are well-established and need no elaboration here, and for athletes, the upside of quaffing in general is even more pronounced. You think PowerBars give you a nice glucose jolt? Slam down a few quick brewskis and you'll get an instant chemistry lesson in the three-step conversion of methyl alcohol into glycogen. There's a reason for that line-up of 5,700-litre beer trucks at the finish line of the Ironman European Championship in Frankfurt, and it isn't to keep the oompah band happy.

And, finally: You know how elite athletes don't worry too much about three-minute penalties anymore, having discovered that using the time to stretch a little and collect themselves can actually improve their overall times? Well, why not make the aid station meals sit-down affairs? White tablecloths, lightstick candles after sundown, table-side salad prep? If Ironman is eighty percent mental, I can't think of anything that would better prepare the mind for those last difficult miles than a relaxing dinner with fellow competitors, topped off with a short snifter of Hennessey and a choice Montecristo stogie.

3 – What's the biggest problem for Ironman racers other than not dying?

I'll tell you what it is: It's boredom. Mind-numbing, will-sapping tedium. Hawai'i is gorgeous, but when you're dragging your butt along the Queen K at barely the speed of smell, it's just one damned chunk of lava after another.

People play all sorts of weird mental games to keep themselves in the moment. Or out of it, depending upon your point of view. They count stripes in the road, or try to recall all the lyrics to "Louie, Louie," or attempt to resolve intricate scientific conundrums, like, "Why does my left quadriceps feel like I've just been bitten by a great white?"

None of this is necessary, which brings me to this suggestion: Issue every participant an iPod, a Blackberry and a Bluetooth headset.

Think of it: You're running along feeling like Dick Cheney in an aerobics class. You reach down to your belt and suddenly you've got Bob Marley wailing "You can make it if you really try..." right in your ear. Is that motivational or what?

Concerned that friends and family back home don't know how you're doing because Ironman.com is on the fritz and all they can get is an endless loop of Mark Allen doing Guido Sarducci impressions? Call 'em up! Or check in at the office! Or find out how Brad and Angelina are doing! A few years ago when my wife was having a particularly tough time at mile 9 of the run, I filled her in on the O.J. verdict. Boy, did she appreciate that timely update. Properly equipped, though, she wouldn't have to be so dependent on me for news.

Did you know you can play on-line poker on a Blackberry? Tell me there could be a greater rush in this world than going all-in with two-seven off suit while heading down into the Energy Lab.

And, hey...I just thought of something else: You wouldn't have to stop at those chintzy pay phones to call in your food order!

* * *

Next time: Neutralizing the unfair advantage of stronger and faster racers and other ideas for improving Ironman.

Ed. note: If editing a Gruenfeld column for Ironman.com is painful (which it is), "Ironing Out Ironman" set new records in pain management. In one quick and easy-to-read column he managed to piss off virtually the entire no-sense-of-humor triathlon community. "Make it shorter?" asked one reader. "It's an Ironman, it needs to be 140.6 miles." (I don't think they quite got Lee's humor.) Race officials were hardly impressed with his "take music and a phone" idea, while Ironman officials, who banned Chuckie Veylupek from the world championship for years because he took a few sips of beer from a spectator, were none-too-impressed with the concept of a "glass or two of '87 Montrachet."

Oh, and how'd you think PowerBar and Gatorade reacted to the "glorified candy bars and sugar water" comment?

It's a miracle I still have hair – although my wife says it started to go grey after Lee came on board with his column.

ISBN: 978-1-78255-005-1

*Available in book stores and on **www.m-m-sports.com***